Happy birthday, Woods!
With love from your
(older) twin,
Mary Bess

Provincial Matters

PROVINCIAL
MATTERS

Essays by
Mary Bess Whidden

University of New Mexico Press

Albuquerque

Library of Congress Cataloging in Publication
Data

Whidden, Mary Bess, 1936–
    Provincial Matters.

    1. New Mexico—Anecdotes, facetiae, satire,
etc.
2. Whidden, Mary Bess, 1936–   —Anecdotes.
I. Title.
F796.6.W44   1985   978.9   85-8577
ISBN 0-8263-0832-5

Illustrations by Betsy James

Design by Milenda Nan Ok Lee

Most of these pieces appeared in their original
form in *Century: A Southwestern Journal of
Observation and Opinion,* many of them in a
regular department called "Provincial Matters."
"Barking up the Wrong Cottonwood" first
appeared in *New Mexico Magazine.*

For Bess and Edgar

Contents

Foreword

For Mary Bess Whidden, humor isn't the sort of thing one writes to establish a literary reputation. Although her essays are masterfully composed, brilliant in word play, and even exhibit the dignity of restraint in a luxurious sort of way, she maintains she has always written them "just for fun." Hers is a natural, almost reflexive, humor, a personal way of dealing with the world, a way of being happy. It is the product of someone who finds life hysterical, "cosmically hysterical," as she says.

In the days before her essays saw print, she would write them for herself and for the private pleasure of her friends. Her rascal humor made people feel good. It caught them by surprise with candy-coated wisecracks, slow-killing satire, a homey skill with puns and double entendres, a Borscht Belt timing with long, pungent jokes. It gave her friends that solid feeling of having their own private genius in their midst. In the early 1980s when Mary Bess's pieces were published by *Century* magazine, a New Mexican bimonthly out of Albuquerque, her happy rascalhood became the private pleasure of a select 10,000 or so who were equally convinced they'd discovered a master in the boondocks. And now with the publication of *Provincial Matters* by the University of New Mexico Press, Mary Bess Whidden should become for many thousands more the gentle, outrageous, self-deprecating scream she is.

Mary Bess started writing for *Century* in May 1981. It was the first time her essays had been published. Of the magazine's seventy-four issues—it folded in October 1983—forty contained her work. With pieces like "Get a Tuffet," "Dear Nanny," "Pac-Man Pox," "A Mavis Foster Day," " 'Twas Brillig in the Soup du Jour," "Abscess Lorraine," and "Junk Mail Junkie," her humor became one of the hallmarks of *Century*'s editorial success. All but one of the essays in this volume were first published in the magazine's opening section called "Provincial Matters," an assortment of appreciations of New Mexico and observations of the passing scene. Mary Bess, along with *Century*'s 250 other writers, photographers, and graphic artists, contributed to the magazine without payment.

In the *Century* days, Mary Bess was a mysterious character. People didn't know who she was, or even who she ought to be. Although the biographical note at the end of her first nine essays proclaimed her to be "an associate professor of English at the University of New Mexico," readers soon forgot, attaching their memory instead to Mary Bess's inspired notion of describing the author of her pieces as a "yodeling waitress and mother of 13." Right up to the last issue of *Century,* people would stop me in the market or approach me on the street and ask "Does she really have thirteen children?" As *Century*'s editor, I felt it my duty to tell the truth, but often found myself fudging with an answer like "Well, she isn't a waitress."

Mary Bess really isn't a waitress. She doesn't have thirteen children and she can't yodel. It is true, however, as she wrote in her essay "Waitress on Wry," that waitresses do invariably ask "Do you want *another* beer?" even when it's her first one. I've heard it with my own ears. And, indeed, Mary Bess really is an associate professor of English at UNM. She's been teaching Shakespeare, Ovidian and Petrarchan poetry, and expository (or, as she says, "suppository") writing, among other things, since 1963. Her students have told me more times than I can count that she's the best teacher they've ever had.

Mary Bess hails from San Angelo, Texas. Someone told me once that her real name wasn't Mary Bess at all, that she'd dreamed it up when she crossed the New Mexico state line, hoping to confuse people into calling her Mary Bell, or Mary Mount, or Mary Mary, or whatever other contrary misnaming they might bumble into. But that theory is inconsistent with Mary Bess's character. Her humor is never cruel, though it's often unkind; it's always directed at herself, but sometimes through the foibles of others; it's never a trap to "getcha," but often makes you laugh at yourself while laughing at her. No, I think Mary Bess is Mary Bess's real name. And I know she received her B.A. from the University of Texas, summa cum laude in 1957; her M.A. in 1959 from the University of North Carolina with a thesis on "The Wit and Humor of Thomas Fuller"; and her Ph.D. from the University of Texas in 1965 with a dissertation entitled "Shakespeare's *Venus and Adonis* and the English Petrarchists." I also know her degrees have little or nothing to do with how funny she is. Mary Bess is congenitally droll. She can't help herself, though much of her humor does rest on her almost infallible skill with prose—an attribute possessed as infrequently by academics as by waitresses.

Being Mary Bess's editor was like being a dolphin's diving coach. I was almost superfluous. I always knew that even if her essays came in five minutes before deadline I'd have nothing to worry about, so beautifully crafted they invariably would be. The high point of *Century*'s Wednesday late-night deadline and copy conference was when managing editor Jim Rini and I settled down to write the title for Mary Bess's pieces. Jim was the best at it. A great gag writer–cartoonist, he could usually track down in the copy the exact phrase or metaphor that gave the piece its special mana. Sometimes a line of his own would come to him while he was dipping french fries into catsup. Other nights we'd spend an hour or more fussing for the right stuff only to find once again that Mary Bess had buried the title like an Easter egg waiting to be found. Those were happy times, indeed.

But then, again, it's hard not to be happy with Mary Bess. She's meticulous with her friendships and an arch companion. She wears floor-length red-and-white polka-dot neckties to lunches at swank restaurants where editors with trade-outs take authors who write for free. She drives you around small parking lots in her U.S.S. *New Jersey*–class Oldsmobile with its plush Blue Boy blue upholstery, its flowery wood-carved plastic panels, its banks of automatic windows, and ice chest of Pearl Beer in the trunk. Her conversation will lead you to believe she really does have a dog named Terd. On occasion, business letters will arrive at your office with the salutation "Dear Precious Sainted Angel." And if you're out on the town with Mary Bess, total strangers will say almost monumentally funny things within earshot. At dinner one night, for instance, after I had failed to interview her for this foreword, Mary Bess and I overheard a large man alone at a separate table put the make on another lone eater, with tomato-blond tresses, across the way. An animated, long distance conversation, it was filled with every cliché of the stalker's art, and one fine originality: "I've been in fashion for three years," the large pursuer purred as he spread his résumé before him, luring the one with tresses to join him for dessert. It was a religious moment when Mary Bess whispered in reverence "Three years, uh?", her eyes raised in gratitude for having received yet another revelation from That Which *Is* Cosmically Hysterical. She made a believer out of me that night, or perhaps I should say reconverted me for the hundredth time—for with Mary Bess the Machine of the Cosmos somehow always manages to justify her faith in the antic majesty of this and that.

—V. B. Price

Unhallowed Nights

Yet again institutions are showing that they can spoil just about anything they touch. On Halloween bank employees work solemnly dressed as clowns, hobos, or ghosts. Dentists perform root canals while marginally disguised as vampires, and supermarkets require clerks to paint themselves as ghouls or to wear fright wigs.

Children on that day march politely to doors with their parents, smile like corporate executives, and thrust forward UNICEF cups. Operating only during the twilight hours, they dress in flame-resistant store-bought clothing less fanciful than the costumes ordinary adults wear dancing on weekends.

In my day as dusk faded on Halloween,

2   children sneaked out of their houses in the
sincerely grotesque outfits we had spent a month
assembling. To avoid making us lie, our parents
pretended ignorance of our stealth and never
asked where we were going. They knew: Sulfur
Draw, a dark, sunken marsh forbidden to us after
nightfall.

There on Halloween the younger children
suffered the ecstasy of being scared witless by
the big boys and girls. Ritual was the key. The
older children stood around a candle and
confessed to the murders they had performed
that week. Every tale could hold up today as a
model of suspense and rising action fleshed out
with a multitude of grisly, marrow-freezing
details. At the end of each narrative the speaker
singled out a smaller child and dedicated the
murder to him. The honored one walked
trembling alone to the candle, where he repeated
the name of the victim and received in his hand
the still soft and moist heart of a sheep or goat.

Following the stories and dedications, we sat
to whisper our plans of vandalism. From the
brush along the river slowly appeared the dead,
murder victims searching for their hearts. Eyes
wild, face and hair clotted with blood, they
moaned and strode woodenly with arms
outstretched until they found their hearts. Each
dead person directed a ghastly gaze at the child

who held his heart, retrieved it, and said, "Now I can rest." For a moment he bowed his head serenely, but then he shrieked to the stars and croaked, "But you shall never rest, you who have held my heart. A curse upon all your days! My spirit will haunt you every minute of your pitiful life." The dead stalked back to the river.

The smaller children thought of this ceremony with sweet terror and pride in their bravery at not having wet their pants. Any psychic scars we carry today come from wounds inflicted in arithmetic class or physical education, not from Sulfur Draw on this night unsullied by grownups.

Murderers, the dead, and the younger children reunited in conspiracy to plot our tricks. No one ever considered the desirability of treats, and certainly mischief was our m.o. and aim.

We did vile acts to property. Although we respected cars too much to harm them, anything else was fair. We spread salt on flower beds. We trailed sheep and goat entrails across doorways. We poured vegetable soup on porches and left notes saying, "My last act on earth was to vomit on your porch. My dead soul will be back to cause you great harm. Beware." We stuffed large boxes with rags soaked in kerosene and lit them in the middle of streets, and as they burned we would ring doorbells and one of us would scream repeatedly, "My baby is inside that box! A curse

4   upon this neighborhood." We tossed a live chicken through the town grouch's back door. Around the chicken's neck was tied a note written in blood: "I am the spirit of your dead ancestors. If you sell me or give me away or wring my neck or pluck me and eat me, you will die. Keep me in your house and be nice to me, or you will be covered with sores and die." If I could be sure of the statute of limitations for juvenile delinquency, I would divulge more.

Annual nights of lawless pranks did not encourage any of us to pursue a criminal career. On the contrary, they calmed us down considerably. A Halloween in Austin when I was ten accounts for my being such a good citizen today. Having abandoned my master plan to fill the mailbox at the Governor's Mansion with mashed potatoes because of the bright lights and guards, I struck at the house of Ma Ferguson, a former governor who served after her husband, Pa, had a brush with impeachment. Her political career was over years before my birth, but I carried a fuzzy image of her as emblematic of all that was tacky and corrupt.

The moment I had taken care of her mailbox with the special energy and adroitness that mischief brings, the porch light came on, and I ran. Soon I heard sirens. I knew that I would be caught and put in the electric chair and that all the lights in town would dim at the instant I fried.

Lying under an oleander listening to the sirens, terrified of my imminent death: For the first and last time I fully understood existentialism. The situation too grave for prayers of simple deliverance, I bargained with the deity and all his staff, vowing over and over never again to find myself on the wrong side of the law. Since my miraculous escape I have kept the bargain and have stayed away from crime, serious crime anyway, despite a great talent for forgery.

For a time after I reached maturity I tried to spur children on to enjoy a real Halloween. They scorned my chicken bones in envelopes which read, "These are the fingers of my last victims. You are next." They refused my offer of dachshunds to carry as their rats, and they ignored my instructions to shout, "Don't step on my snake!" Nothing scary finds a place in their adult-monitored protocol.

If banks, dentists, supermarkets, and parents who side with institutions would stay out of the act, children could have one unhallowed night for themselves. Today's children parading through a sanitized Halloween miss out on firsthand encounters with an invited gothic terror. Probably they have to find their fears on the flickering screen or, worse, in real life.

Dog Days at the Mail Box

A magazine recently printed an author's query welcoming "personal anecdotes that shed light on the dog/human relationship in any part of the world." Here is the plea of someone desperate for mail, bags and bags of mail, more mail than arrives at the Publishers Clearing House at Sweepstakes time.

Possibly this querying author has a darker motive such as wanting to study the syntactical oddities of all kinds of people. He may, however, be a forthright student of his topic but an innocent like me who doesn't know what he's asking for. Being of a rustic simplicity and wanting one summer to house-sit near the Huntington Library, I placed an ad in the Los Angeles papers: "Professional woman will stay in your house and do anything. Free." The replies,

8   none having to do with watering plants or paying the maid and gardener, would make a snappy chapter on bizarre erotic fantasies of Southern California. The dog scholar will get even more, though surely less colorful, letters than I did.

Some will be ordinary. "Cute, cute, what can I tell you? At night she puts away her little playtoys." "You have to know about Merlin—not really a dog, but a cat WHO THINKS HE'S A DOG!" And others:

Dear Professor,

My boyfriend Dennis has a dog. Dennis dont pay him hardly no mind, just lets him lay outside in hot and cold and talks rough to him and even kicks him if hes mad. When we get in the pickup Terd (thats his name) jumps in the back and Dennis dont care if hes thirsty or hungry or falls out. Now professor this here is a good dog who dont bite or nothing and minds real good, and Dennis treats him like dirt. Sometimes I feel like Terd the way Dennis treats me. Youve got to tell me what to do. I wont do nothing till I hear from you. I feel like your the only friend I have in the world.

Love, Wyvonne
Star Route 3
Belleville, Oklahoma

Dear Beautiful Person:

Cosmic Wombat, a
German shepherd cross,
experiences the All, like
perfect, no hangups. He
has his own mantra and
everything, you know,
and when we smoke he
gets mystical like you
wouldn't believe. He
has never tasted
animal flesh. At 6
a.m. and 4 p.m.
he does yoga with
us, just a few
positions he's
comfortable with.
You know where

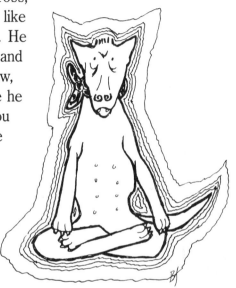

he's coming from. He's into authenticity, you
know, and empathy like you wouldn't believe.
When his old lady had a litter he *delivered* the
pups, licked them clean and everything, you
know. He respects the land, digs not digging,
you know.

If you are a Good Person and want to see him,
bring 3 morning glory seeds, 9 dried beans, and
a 6-inch leather thong and come join us. Like we
know the mixed-up university scene you're in,

10   and we can give you space and mind-blowing
serenity like you wouldn't believe.

Love, love, love from all of us,
Mushroom
Sunshine
Cornstalk
Andrew Carnegie Mellon Grass
MANDALA RAMSHAH
Telluride, Colo

Dear Dr. Smith:

My dog saved my life! I was on the way out of
the house for a conference with my daughter's
teacher when my neighbor came to tell me that
Ben, our Old English sheepdog, had chewed up
her newest copy of the *Begonia Crier* she had
left on her lawn chair. She followed me through
the house to find Ben for a scolding. In the
laundry room we startled the cat, who jumped
onto the ironing board and knocked the iron
down on my neighbor's foot. I ran to call the
emergency number because I could see that the
small bones were crushed, and I ran right into
Ben who had been flushed out of hiding by my
neighbor's screams. He turned back into the
pantry shelves, knocking down 36 jars of apricot
jam, 12 of which shattered on my neighbor, and
Ben ran like crazy out the back door through my

neighbor's garden (just a week before the flower show, too, and my neighbor had won several ribbons the year before) and through her greenhouse, collapsing it. Had Ben not detained me from the teacher's conference I would have been in my station wagon on the bridge the instant it was washed out! He saved my life! If you are giving out medals or anything, Ben should get one!

Frances Hunnicutt
12 Aimee Semple McPherson Lane
Akron, Ohio

[Page 1 of this letter is missing. Page 2 begins:]

peed right there in front of all my business associates and their wives. I don't need to tell you that my own little woman was so mortified she would have peed herself except old Charley here made light of the situation and said, "I gave him some carpet cleaner to drink an hour ago and he's just doing his job." Well, everyone got a big kick out of that.

I'm sure you won't hear about any other dog who knew how to get attention like Buster and I know you won't hear about a situation that would have been so embarrassing if old Charley here hadn't been on his old toes.

12   Nice talking to you and can't wait to hear we
took the prize.

> Charles M. Nichols
> Apex Carpet Cleaners
> Omaha, Nebraska

P.S. If you're ever out this way, give us a call.
We get to New York City for the conventions,
and next time your missus and mine can do some
shopping and we can all take in a show.

Dear Mister Professor,

Wilber, the smartest blue tick hound dog in the
county, has lived with me for a long time now.
One day a few years back he brought to the
house six baby rabbits, carrying them one by one
with the easiest mouth
you ever saw. He acted
just like he was they
mama. If I was late
getting they dinner
he'd come push me
behind the knees and
then trot to they
box, whining like he
never did for his own
dinner. Them bunny
rabbits fattened up
and grew tall. I'd

put them out in my garden and they'd stand up to nibble at the greens. Whenever one of them commenced to hop out of the garden Wilber would nose it back and scold it with the funniest sound you ever did hear—like a big stomach growling. He'd even hep me carry them back to the box, still with that easy mouth.

One Monday morning only five of them was in they box, the lid was on, wasn't no way the one could have gotten out. The next day just four, and ever day down to none. They was just about big enough for me to let loose anyway, but I worried some. I thought here I have myself a mystery and I let the box stay thinking my neighbor might come by and help me figure out how they got away.

Wellsir the next week I heard some sounds from the box and sure enough they was a family of five little newbornded bunny rabbits, and Wilber set in being they mama. It took me rearing three families of bunny rabbits and watching Wilbur blow up fat and go back to skinny to figure out what he was up to. Ever after I've been taking one out for my own stew. I'm telling you that for a long spell Wilber thought I was one dumb white man.

I can send you a snapshot with one of my next letters. I'm sending you a couple of goodluck

14 charms and can give you a whole lot more of them. Write me real soon.

Haskell Ordway
Parsons Ridge, Tennessee

Vet's Met
The Coves, R.I.

Dear Professor Dr. Smith:

I do not make a practice of answering the queries of authors, though I did provide assistance in a similar situation some years ago by recounting in detail an unfortunate (and unforgivable) incident in which Noel Coward was viciously rude toward the aunt and uncle of a dear friend of mine. Nonetheless, I saw fit to oblige you because your research seems sincere and significant and because I can be of real help.

For your study you should know of our apricot poodle, Bubbles, whom we named for Beverly Sills, the operatic soprano. Bubbles, like the great lady for whom she was named, sings.

My seamstress has fashioned little costumes for Bubble's best roles—Carmen and Mimi, of course, and a divine Madame Butterfly. My husband, a wag, often observes that she looks more like Madame Moth, but that's not so, as he well knows. Her finest appearance—and we never allow her to parade before strangers, only our dearest friends of whom we are fortunate to number many—is as the Queen of the Night. She stands on her hindmost feet and reaches the notes as we play from our excellent collection of operatic recordings. Her sense of tempi is extraordinary, as is her dramatic skill. She is truly a gifted performer, and we are deeply grateful that she does not lean toward the Wagnerian. We do not customarily permit persons other than the closest of friends to attend her recitals, but you, because of your interest, would be warmly welcome to motor out for her next. We shall send you a programme. I can't know whether you appreciate beautiful stage settings, but hers are magnificent, I assure you.

We should like to ask one tiny favor of you: In your correspondence you may discover a talented male dog, a tenor (not a hound of any variety! We have already suffered through that humiliating experience). We should very much like to have him, if he has a true talent, at our Holiday Entertainment, to which you, as I

16   have indicated, would be most welcome, as
would the owners and/or musical trainers of the
tenor. We await your courteous reply.

Sincerely yours,
Mrs. Vergil Ovid Smacks

Dear Professor Smith:
    You may have a soft spot for dogs, as I once
did, but I swear to you I know one Old English
Sheepdog I am going to kill as soon as I can get
around again. My only fear is that I may lack the
nerve to fracture the feet of that miserable
owner of his.

Not A Dog Lover
14 Aimee Semple McPherson Ln
Akron, Ohio

Dear Prof. Smith,
    Eric, the dachshund, does anything he likes,
and if I try to prevent him or correct him he
bites me. He takes the dinner off the table. He

destroys my guests' leather gloves, even taking them from overcoats. He goes into their purses and destroys lipsticks, compacts, pill boxes, and contact lenses, he empties the cabinets and dresser drawers, he chews up books and magazines, sofas and mattresses, electrical cords (I unplugged everything three years ago), and anything else.

He has never made an attempt to be housebroken. When I put him out he climbs the stairs to the roof, and then people stop and come to the door and say, "There's a dog on your house."

I have never had such good company, have never known anyone else so interesting and full of life, and have never loved anything so much in my life. When he looks me in the eye, he shows he knows me.

Yours,
Gladys Potter
(no return address)

18   Dear Mr. Smith,

Folly is sweet and happy. She came to us when she was a puppy and has never done anything wrong. She wants only to please. I love her. I want her to have a long and happy life.

Wishing you the same,
Mary Bess Whidden
Albuquerque, New Mexico

Course Offerings

Legislators and real people can work themselves into a good panic conjuring up horrors that might go on in state universities. They fear that professors are teaching moral depravity, nonsense, or subversive political attitudes. Then these good folk make a leap of faith so great that they believe that what is being taught is also being learned.

The anxiety level of the public is low, however, compared with the edginess within the universities themselves. Internal scrutiny, which has unfortunate anatomical connotations, is severe and constant. Watchdog committees monitor committees who oversee curriculum committees whose business is to police course

20   offerings. Everyone is jumpy about the possibility
of a class that sounds trendy, nonacademic, not
up to standards.

   With the collusion of its chairman, I once
planted a list of fake projected courses before a
committee of high-minded faculty members
(redundant, I know). Outrage, fury, and threats
so overcame the group that I had to confess long
before the reading was complete. Their
testiness, not to say gullibility, showed me what I
should have known all along. As signs in airports
say about bombs, curriculum is no joking matter.
Here are the courses anyway.

   INNER SURFING. Tank Tankersley, instructor,
Ripple Health Spa. This seminar will study
surfing in all its aspects from all points of view.
Films will illustrate the ecstasy of riding the Big
One in harmony with the self, the board, and
nature. The class will take two field trips to
Elephant Butte.

   OLD TIMES IN NEW MEXICO. Sarah T. Otis,
instructor. Mrs. Sarah T. Otis, resident of
Lincoln County since 1898, will share her
memories of a New Mexico girlhood. Her father
was postmaster for 34 years and was the first in
the county to raise Rhode Island Reds. For 44

years her mother was corresponding secretary of
the Skip-Like-A-Bunny Sewing Circle. Her family
owned the first stereopticon in New Mexico and
had many vivid experiences: a hound dog who
sucked eggs, a grass fire, traditional festivities at
Christmas and Thanksgiving. Not only will Mrs.
Otis lecture on these events at length, but also
she will show to the class such memorabilia as
her first dance card and, to illustrate the
lawlessness of children coming of age in
Territorial New Mexico, a record of her first
library fine. Reading list: "My Diary," Sarah T.
Otis [unpublished].

A TRIBUTE TO ELVIS. Gretchen Kirk, Professor
Emerita of Music, and Mary Bess Whidden, Elvis
expert, instructors. A thorough examination of
the art, life, and loves of the great musical genius
of this century. Each week the class will hear
selected renditions by the artist, comparing and
contrasting his various versions of many songs.
This course will explore the artist's development
chronologically and will relate it to events in his
life. Reading list: *My Time With Elvis*, Lolita Lola
as told to Elmer Coates; *Our Graceland Gang*,
Colonel Parker as told to Zelma Rutledge Crimp;
The King, Zeke Luke Heron; *An Elvis
Scrapbook*, eds. Colonel Parker, et al.; *The*

National Enquirer, many issues in the private collections of the instructors.

DOING YOUR OWN THING. Deans of all Colleges, instructors. A laid-back survey of the autonomy of the self and of our responsibilities to self-direction in every area of life. We shall discuss in a leisurely manner ways of combating those hostile forces—institutional, bureaucratic,

economic—which attempt to make us conform to   23
the work ethic and to other attitudes counter to
self-knowledge and self-expression. Students who
enroll should already have found their own things
and should have anti-establishment convictions. If
we decide to do drugs the class will meet off-
campus. Anything goes. Attendance is not
required.

THE ZEN EXPERIENCE OF MAKING MONEY ON
THE MALL. Tulip Birdwing and Sundance Lewis,
instructors. A deep experiencing of the spiritual
growth inherent in marketing on campus. We'll
be into socks, jewelry, roller-skate rental,
macramé, and shirts, always considering the
contributions sales and exchanges make to the
oversoul and to our own inner serenity.

COUNTRY AND WESTERN DANCING. Bobby Jim
Curtis and Ormalu Hicks, instructors. This
course demands academic excellence at every
turn. Students will master the art and symbology
of the two-step, the lurch, and the dip. There
will be several difficult examinations and a
research paper as well as a public recital.
(Instructors' note: "This here ain't no barn dance
this here is school.")

MAKING IT WITHOUT MATH. Cylvia Cypher,

24   instructor. Too often we are compelled to think of the world numerically. This course teaches effective ways of living in the modern age without doing even simple calculations, and students will learn the futility of mathematical concepts and formulations. A reading knowledge of English is not required but might come in handy.

WHY POLICE? COPING WITH COPS. Champ Higgins and Rocky Ruggles, instructors. Police brutality is widespread and is threatening our way of life. This class will first of all learn methods of evading and fighting the fuzz. Then the course will address the question of the need for police at all. Guest panelists will include members of the Hell's Angels and the governor, who has consented to speak on both sides of the issue. Anyone who cares about the future of this nation and its present social structure may participate in the final session of the course, a rally to be held in a shopping center. Reading list: *Burn, Baby, Burn,* Anon. as told to Anon.

My Car

It is a truth universally acknowledged that a student left to choose his own composition topic will produce an essay entitled "My Car." Written with ardor, it leads to an improbable, maudlin moral.

A man sizing up someone or renewing a friendship asks, "What kind of car do you drive?" The answer probably makes little difference, but the question inches toward intimacy. Asked how they are, many people answer with descriptions of the ails of their cars. I have heard one adult greet another with "Hello! How's your car?"

A loyal American, I'm the last to suggest that we entertain an obsession with our machines. In this country we care about books, art, music, planetary harmony, equality of social and

26   economic opportunity, education, and decent
veterinary treatment for our pets.

As a brief respite from straining at these
primary concerns, today let us each take
typewriter in hand and devote a few minutes to
the activity that releases students from their
tensions—tapping out a brief description of our
car. Nostalgia about ones from the past won't do.
I could weep over the red topless Jeep I pushed
into a lot to sell; a Studebaker that stopped only
if the tires nudged onto a curb; a venerable Nash
named Winged Victory that made into a bed; and
an ecru Mustang that gave way to the only new
car I ever owned, the world's most beautiful
sculpture which, on its 2,000-mile check-up, was
wrecked by the garage. No, to play by the rules
we must write "My Car." I get to go first.

A couple of years ago I found myself relying
upon public transportation, though I don't know
why it's called public since I was the only one
using it. The bus doesn't work for westerners. It
doesn't go where we want to go, and it removes
our sense of control, conquest, adventure,
autonomy, and risk.

So I went shopping. Since I prefer to allot my
money to the dentist and other charitable
institutions, I had very little to spend, but I
restricted myself to rhapsodic ads, avoiding those
which ended "runs good." In every instance the

prose outdid the product. Three had no
windshields, one no windows at all. Two were
fine except for needing transmissions, and four
sat in ponds of opalescent fluid. One prize—I
could see myself zipping around the country in
it—had the muffler and what very well might
have been the carburetor on the back seat.
Others were missing various essential entrails.
One had "totaled" written on the accident report
in the glove compartment. These were out of my
price range.

The car I cottoned to was painted many
different day-glo colors, had an ornamental fringe
around each window and fur on the dashboard
and a lurid approximation of *The Last Supper* on
the passenger door. It rested on blocks, the
owner doubted that he wanted to sell, and he
didn't have the papers.

A friend arranged with her neighbors for the
sale of what is now My Car, an Oldsmobile 98
which would be registering for the draft if it were
human. Everyone I know drives a shiny car that
would fit neatly into the trunk of My Car. In the
first flush of excitement at seeing a car as big as
an ocean liner, four full-grown men stretched out
in that trunk with room left for several cases of
beer. They didn't seem at all upset at being left
there for the evening.

Equipped with power windows, power

28   everything, My Car has a grandeur, a bent
dignity. A proud relic from another age, it sails
along impervious to the scorn of those who hold
it personally responsible for draining our supply
of fossil fuel and for any trouble we may be
having with OPEC. Young men in Japanese cars
running on vacuum cleaner engines give My Car
an ancient hand symbol, and I hear derision from
Volvos bearing signs, "Save the Whales" and "I'd

rather be reading John Milton."

I like to think that My Car represents a kind of recycling, a holdout against contrived obsolescence. With luck we will all survive beyond the fashion. If we take more space than we need to turn a corner, if our design reminds the young of a past that seems ostentatious and carefree, then I hope they can learn from us and park alongside with understanding and amity.

On the Road Again

The New Mexico driving test has entered the modern world. Although it is still called a "written" test, no longer are grown people bent in old school desks chewing the ends of state-owned pencil stubs and erasing with care not to rub through the paper. Gone are the diagrams, Matisse-like in their clarity and simplicity, of roads and cars.

Instead the Motor Vehicle Department has rows of upright machines which display striking color photographs of Santa Fe, especially of La Fonda and the cathedral, and lights spell out questions having nothing to do with the scenes. Space-age sounds alert the players when to push the buttons of their choice.

When I went for my new license, a few young

32 men were idling away the afternoon holding the
machines with locked elbows, jostling them as if
they were pinball games and apparently gambling.
All the machines but mine (number 8) flashed the
correct answer after every miss, but mine left
me with only a punitive buzz and lights flashing
WRONG, so I can repeat the test as I remember it
but not the correct answers.

1. Stopping at a red light is
    a. illegal
    b. dangerous
    c. peculiar.

2. Drinking while driving is
    a. mandatory
    b. customary
    c. optional before 5 p.m.

3. If your vehicle begins to spin
    a. you are on La Bajada
    b. you have ten days to do your
       Christmas shopping
    c. try to remember the name of the Lone
       Ranger's horse and shout "heigh-ho."

4. A stop sign means
    a. accelerate
    b. three fatal accidents have recently

occurred at that intersection
c. your brakes don't work.

5. Drag racing is
    a. expressly forbidden under code 26a,
       427
    b. a sport the whole family can enjoy
    c. fun if your wife's clothes are prettier
       than yours.

6. An unbroken yellow line in your lane
   means
    a. jaundice
    b. the painting crews are on their toes
    c. you are heading in the wrong direction.

7. Turn signals are
    a. clues in a game in which you guess
       when the other vehicle will hit you
    b. ornaments on all the new cars
    c. illegal.

8. A U-turn is
    a. handy if you want to turn around
    b. required in Española
    c. a plumbing tool.

9. A yield sign means
    a. nothing

    b. you should put your vehicle in reverse gear

    c. you should think about "*i* before *e* except after *c* or when pronounced like *a* in *neighbor* or *weigh*."

10. Most accidents happen
    a. when the couple is truly in love
    b. during high-speed police chases
    c. in the home.

11. A left turn is
    a. certain death
    b. a good way to annoy the people behind you
    c. different in some respects from a right turn.

12. How high are vehicles allowed to be?
    a. 14 feet, 7 inches
    b. pretty tall if there are no underpasses
    c. the equivalent of 15 beers or 8 joints.

13. Auto emission standards are
    a. not discussed in mixed company
    b. fads in California
    c. making automobile manufacturers go broke.

14. You should stop for pedestrians at a cross-walk
    a. if you're in that kind of mood
    b. at peril of your life
    c. to tell them they have no business walking.

15. Driving defensively means
    a. wearing a helmet and full body cast and having inflatable bags
    b. having a chip on your shoulder
    c. being on the lookout for Texas plates.

I passed, probably because number 8 was on the blink, but my moment came before the camera when the shutter snapped just as I read a sign pasted at eye-level, "REMBER, A SMILE EMPROVES YOU'RE IMAGE," and I gaped in grammatical terror. For four years grocery clerks will see my picture, a silent movie actress recoiling, aghast at meeting the inevitable.

Valentines *Perdu*

Last week as I wandered through a drugstore—I do drugstores the way others do drugs—and noticed the greeting-card section suddenly bright red, I harked back to the day in the third grade when I opened a pack of fifty valentines to address to my friends. The cards were cheerful and entertaining, but they all said, "To My Teacher."

I gave one to Miss Liston, the severe dictator who maintained declared warfare with me in the classroom every day and was hired, I believed, to ruin the third grade. I was happy to give the other five teachers in the school a card apiece. Mrs. Hofstetter, a large gelid woman in black who visited our school once a month to teach us that we could never understand the complex

38   relation between Re and Fa, looked
      inconvenienced and less than ever like Maria Von
      Trapp when I handed her the greeting. Later she
      told my mother that my valentine was the only
      one she had ever received. To my violin teacher,
      Mrs. Miller, I gave three. I delivered one to my
      sister's piano teacher, and I walked to the high
      school and left one for each of her regular
      teachers. Any academic success I later had
      resulted from this thoughtfulness.

      My bounty had just begun when I learned to
      expand the definition of "teacher." Tom Green
      County Public Library employed three librarians,
      whose sole task was to keep me away from the
      adult section. Since the day they had
      apprehended me crawling out a back window with
      a stack of reference books, their job descriptions
      narrowed to pre-scolding me. After I offered up
      their valentines, they turned from police work to
      encouraging use of my borrowing privileges to
      the point of letting me take home overnight the
      C volume of an encyclopedia.

      The court house, a WPA version of the
      Parthenon, was a haunt of mine as I considered
      myself important to Democratic Party politics, so
      I presented a valentine to Judge Curtsinger and
      to all the workers in the County Clerk's Office. I
      gave teacher-valentines to salesladies in the
      department store and the owner of our grocery

store. The man with the parrot at the feed store posted his on the wall.

The owners of both drugstores were so moved that they gave my friends and me license to sit on the floor all summer and read comic books without buying. Last year I went into one of these drugstores to buy some thirty-year-old postcards and found it unrecognizable except for the bracing aroma that small drugstores have. As impoverished, dusty, and desperate as the apothecary shop in *Romeo and Juliet,* it had a few stale items for sale, and the fountain, closed a decade before, was shrouded. When I told the owner my name, he said, "You know, I've always thought that someday you'd walk in here and buy this place."

Of all the eccentrics in town, the crankiest was a fat man who ran the shoe-repair store on my beat in the business district. He liked the valentine I handed him and the ones I inscribed with the names of my friends and slipped under his door. For the rest of his life he told customers that he couldn't tolerate most people but children sure took a shine to him.

The postman, the school janitor, the woman who took tickets and kept order at the Angelus theater, the man who sat all day in an easy chair on the sidewalk in front of his furniture store, and Mrs. Runkels, the egg lady, strained ever

40   after to impart to me minor lessons in life. One I have yet to understand: "If anyone gives you a quarter, don't give back five nickels."

After such a heady time with Valentine's Day I lost interest in the holiday apart from the ritualistic purchase of cellophane sacks of tiny heart-shaped inedibles with messages on them. But this year, misty with these reveries of a holiday that gives time off work to no one, I sent a valentine to my first-grade teacher at Mirabeau B. Lamar School with a note thanking her for teaching me to read.

My memory probably conflates weeks into one stunning instant, an awakening as dazzling and immediate as the miracle of Annie Sullivan's pupil, who felt water running over her hand from the pump at the same time the word was spelled out on her arm and called out, "Wahhhw." In my version, Miss Gibbs held up a big card with the letter M, a picture she had drawn of a cow, and the word "MOO." She said, "M has the sound of MOO," and I could read.

As soon as the valentine dropped into the mail slot, I began to agonize over what I had written. Since the moment of learning, real or imagined, had been blazing in intensity for me, the egocentricity of a first grader led me to believe that Miss Gibbs remembered it too. Instead of saying, "Thank you for teaching me to read," I wrote insanely, "Thank you for the MOO that opened up the universe." I considered throwing a stick of dynamite into the mailbox, driving all night to intercept the card at the other end, calling her to say that I had inadvertently mailed her the wrong card. Otherwise, the local papers were bound to herald in millennium type: "ANGELO GIRL ARRESTED FOR TORMENTING LIDA GIBBS." (At my death, if the *San Angelo Standard-Times* thinks to record it, the headline will read, "Angelo Girl Dies At 114.")

This morning the postman delivered to me a letter in firm Palmer script, with the salutation, "My dear First Grade Baby." Among gracious acknowledgments of my gratitude appeared this passage: "Your account of the M lesson brought back fond memories of my early teaching days. One incident I recall about those letter cards was when I asked all children whose names began with S to come to the front. Bubba Hughes raced up to me. I asked if Bubba started with the S sound. He, rascal that he was, said, 'I fooled you that time, Miss Gibbs. My name is Studley Emory Hughes.' "

Next year I'm giving fifty valentines to my teachers.

Junk Mail Junkie

We all tend to correspondence, and I love to write letters—to the wrong people. I gather my equipment and settle down to give news to friends languishing in foreign lands, to write urgently required notes of thanks, and to tell relatives I am thinking of them. However, my attention soon roams to a stack of unsolicited mail. The letters below will go out tomorrow with my signature.

Dear Sombrero Café,
  You were very kind to send me the menu for your take-out restaurant. Frankly I probably will not participate in your gala opening coupon extravaganza since I'd rather not take out anything I could more comfortably take in, and I

44   have my favorite places already, chiefly the
Sanitary Tortilla Factory. Your menu, consisting
mainly of nachos, makes me think you might be
interested in a historical note: I met Nacho!

Years ago I used to visit *la familia de mi amigo*
(the family of my friend) in Eagle Pass, Texas.
We would go across the river to Piedras Negras
to see Nacho, who sold food to *la madre de mi
amigo* (the mother of my friend). *Un día* (one
day) *la señora* (the mother of my friend) asked
Nacho to prepare something *especial* (special) for
a *fiesta* (party), and he invented NACHOS.

You will want to know that that Nacho used
only *tostados* (corn chips), *queso* (cheese), and
jalapeños (tiny peppers), never *refritos* (beans). If
your archival integrity is not strong enough to
make you abandon *refritos,* you should tell your
patrons that you serve mutant nachos. If you
want to shake *la mano* (the hand) that shook *la
mano* (the hand) of Nacho, let me know.

Su amiga (your friend)

Dear Congressman:

How lovely of you to think to write me
informing me of issues since I worked so very
hard to defeat you in the last election that I
hardly have breath to campaign against you in the
next. You are sweet to confide in me the shame

of your votes hurting women and children and the poor, but I'm afraid I can be only an attentive listener, not one who can absolve your sins. You ask me to tell you of anything you might do to help me. Please help me put a good Democrat in your place.

Dear Vita-Co,

What a delight to receive your letter showing concern over my "nutritional habits" and the valuable information on supplements! My habits are not nutritional at all, but I am grateful that you took pains to write telling of your personal curiosity about what I eat. Now don't go on worrying about me, silly man. I do fine with orange juice and okra. Your unusual interest is touching, and if your letter is a timid way of asking me to dinner, please call and set a date. I am honored and look forward to telling you about my book—*You Eat What You Are.*

Dear Pest-Erad,

Yesterday I was astonished to find your cruel note accusing me of keeping a house crawling with insects. I don't know what you've heard and can't imagine who might spread such rumors. Whatever caused you to single me out for reproach on such a delicate matter, I must

46   object. No, you are not welcome to inspect my
cupboards and closets, and I'd appreciate not
hearing from you again until you have something
nice to say.

Dear Utilities Company:

Bless your heart for sending the bulletin on
our rate increase. I appreciate your taking the
time to explain the reasons. That little pie with
the colorful slices made everything clear at once.

Please let me intrude upon your busy day to
ask a favor. May I pre-pay my bill to reduce your
interest costs (the green slice of that cute pie)?
I'd also be happy to volunteer my leadership
skills to help you trim some of the big blue piece
for management.

Your partner,

Dear Simeon Medical Mission Fund,

You have my heartiest good wishes for your
endeavor. Since I can't find your disease in my
medical reference books nor your country in the
atlas, I think I'll pass. Surely you can treat this
mysterious illness in that uncharted part of the
world without my aid.

Thank you for the "free gift," which already is
included in my collection of kitsch. Since I am

emphatically non-profit, you can probably write   47
me off, as I do you herewith.

Dear Dr. Armand Hammer,

I received with pleasure your elegant report of
the annual shareholders' meeting of Occidental
Petroleum Corporation. You understand that
distance, not lack of enthusiasm, prevented my
being there. The photograph of a capacity crowd
in the Grand Ballroom of the Beverly Wilshire
Hotel deepens my sadness at having missed the
occasion. Everyone in the picture seems rapt
except for the man on the lower right. I sincerely
hope he has recovered.

The screening of our annual film must have
been thrilling indeed. *Twenty-five Years of Growth,*
a catchy title, and the movie's depiction of "plans
to construct the world's largest open-pit coal
mine" give me hope that it will be in local
theaters soon.

The objectives of the corporation exactly
match my personal ones: "dispose of assets that
do not fit our strategic objectives [have a garage
sale], acquire other assets that complement our
strategic objective [go to garage sales], cut costs
[but there I go making reckless promises],
improve capital management [balance the
checkbook], and substantially enhance

48   productivity in all our lines of business [stop being lazy]."

Your next section, however fresh and forceful the metaphor, worries me: "This restructuring process is painful and a tragedy for those fine people whose jobs will be a casualty of the program and we regret this immensely. However, all of this is part of the necessary pruning process to permit resumed growth and resumed record profitability. Even the strongest, healthiest oak tree [here you're in full poetic gear] requires pruning and shaping from time to time."

Forgive me if I fret about the discarded limbs. I pray with all my heart that pruning will not include the distinguished members of the board with annual salaries that could buy my neighborhood. These men make important decisions, and I hate to see them go. But if the choice is between them and the people whose livelihoods depend on our Oxy, then let the tree surgeons have at them. I lament the tragedy of the fine board members, a casualty of the program.

Because it has literary merit and is not cluttered with arithmetic, the annual report is exceptionally entertaining this year. A warming note (Heavens, I'm mixing metaphors when your

report is so good as to stick with the one it has)
begins the document: "At the Chairman's
suggestion, which was enthusiastically received,
the meeting began with the Pledge of Allegiance
to the Flag." Why, oh why, Dr. Hammer, did the
shareholders, after such a reception, later vote
the way they did? "A proposal to provide in the
by-laws that all stockholder meetings commence
with the Pledge of Allegiance to the Flag was
defeated 65,415,694 shares (59.6 percent of the
outstanding capital stock) against and 4,006,193
shares (3.7 percent) in favor." I suspect the
problem lay in some confusion over the meaning
of "commence," don't you?

After you congratulated the "lady shareholder"
who made the Pledge suggestion at last year's
meeting, I wonder that the gentlemen
shareholders didn't go along with it, especially
after your altruism in recommending that we
improve "relations with Mexico so we might get
a better deal on oil from Mexico" and your
optimism that you "expect that one day the
fertilizer business will come back." What a day to
yearn for, Dr. Hammer!

You can bet your life that I'll be at the next
meeting, as I know you will even after the
tragedy of your job's being a casualty of the
program because of pruning oaks. We'll push the

50   Pledge issue and ignore the quibbling of those
      picky people who are "concerned about present
      events in the Middle East and what the effects
      would be with regard to our Libyan operations."
         Meanwhile, maybe I can catch *Twenty-five
      Years of Growth* in Libya or Mexico. (Remind me
      to tell you about the time I met Nacho!)

                                            I love you.
                              MARY BESS WHIDDEN

Barking up the Wrong Cottonwood

When I travel, I boast so ardently about the wonders of New Mexico that occasionally an innocent couple takes me up on my universal invitation to pay a visit. Believing that I live in the place of my description—an ornate and antiquarian portrait that obscures any change since 1820—they arrive at Albuquerque International Airport with a knowledge garnered from my rhapsodies, a close reading of *Death Comes for the Archbishop,* and glances through a few coffee-table books.

As we pass convenience stores on the short drive home, my guests murmur to the verge of whining, their expectations shattered and their feelings hurt. To assuage them and cover my own exotic testimonies, I say, "My, we're glad to have this new little development. You can imagine the nuisance of wandering from horno to horno to buy my daily tortillas and Indian fry bread. Some days I am simply too busy to listen to secret legends or swap recipes and sensitive gazes with curanderas."

The arrival home teaches me that at a certain pitch of hope visitors believe whatever they choose. As I wheel into the driveway of my pink frame-stucco house with a flat roof, they exult, "An adobe hacienda! We knew it would be." "Pueblo style," I skirt. "You'll soon learn to distinguish it from territorial."

Once in the door they look down for the brick floors of their picture books. They have been curious, I know, about whether I had herringbone or Harris tweed or whatever the other patterns are called. "Hardwood," I announce. "This house is special in the state because it has a basement, and the weight of the bricks would . . . you know; and we don't need basements because it rains only in August except in Santa Fe when storms come for the opera season."

By now, bedazzled by the sun and sky, they see exactly what they want to see. They scan the furniture, every piece but one a gift, castoff, or bequest from people who have never lived in New Mexico. They seize on the exception: "A colonial Spanish chair, no, a Taos chair—which?"

"I bought it at a garage sale," I admit, "and experts call it a WPA chair. The history of the WPA and its contribution to local culture is fascinating."

"And this Navajo rug! How elemental yet intricate and mathematically precise! Tell us the symbology." Here I succumb to the limits of honesty: "I bought this one in Juárez. The vendor wanted $25, but I held out for 10." Shunning the truth, one of them interrupts, "It's one of those—what do you call them?" "One Gray Hill," I answer.

"Where are your chiles?" "In the freezer in the basement. Have I told you how lucky I am to have a basement?" "I mean the glorious red strings." "The ristras? I ate them. I ate them this morning." From embarrassment or admiration they roll their eyes and recoil from the ceiling. "Your beams, the vigas, you've covered them over." "Well, with the solar panel and skylight, I was forced to," I lie. "The sun here is so strong and reliable that on an average day of, say, 874 langleys I don't want to miss the toastiness nature provides."

A discernible chill settles around us, and the time is right for me to confess that freakishly no Pueblo dances occur during the week, the aspen have long since disrobed, and I know nothing about where to find turquoise.

54   All these years I've been barking up the wrong cottonwood. Outrageous and indelicate as it seems, I have decided from this moment on to tell the truth about the lives most of us live here. Taking a clue from New Yorkers who talk about Manhattan as if we knew every street and avenue, henceforth my paeans of New Mexico will proclaim that I live in SoLo (south of Lomas Boulevard), an intellectually sparkling area near Bas Ridgecrest, Haut Ridgecrest being a semihistoric, postwar, quasi-elegant enclave for the near rich. For an adobe fix, we have to leave our own houses, and we drive in cars to gasp at enchanted vistas, though at home we can see the mountains, mesas, volcanoes, and sunsets if we crane our necks out the windows just right.

    Everyone is still welcome to visit. My basement is worth the trip.

Shopping Mad

When I moved to Albuquerque, my chief complaint concerned shopkeepers and their clerks. Occupied with business, they were literal and solemn, staying close to their merchandise and cash registers.

After a life in Texas and the South, where every trip to the post office, bank, or store meant a social encounter, a time for banter and friendship, I was used to the exchange of *mots,* many of them *bon.* Any financial transaction was offhand, beside the point of the visit.

I wish I had kept a letter from my hometown bank sent to me when I was away at school, but at the time it seemed a fairly ordinary business memo. I had bought a Volkswagen for $950 and had written a check with the assurance that,

56   though I had about $25 in my account, the bank
would establish a loan because of my note on the
check, "for new car." No other paper changed
hands, and monthly I sent whatever I could
afford until after a dry spell of two or three
months the letter came: "Dear Mary Bess, If
you don't pay something on your car loan soon,
we will have to call your daddy. Hope everything
is fine with you. Love, San Angelo National
Bank." I remember the letter only because I was
surprised that nice people who ran an office for
visiting would write openly about money.

   Now I yearn for the old days in Albuquerque
when clerks treated customers as fugitives or,
worse, as purchasers, not friends. Clerks were, I
thought then, dull and distant. One of my first
business trips took me downtown (remember
downtown?) to buy tennis balls. The man behind
the counter showed me the best, and I was
disappointed that he was interested in the
product instead of our conversation. "Why, you
can drive a nail into these," he said. "Then I can't
take them," I lamented. "I don't have a hammer."
Betraying our friendship, he explained that I
didn't *have* to drive a nail into them, that he was
demonstrating the quality of the material. After
an impersonal lesson on physics and the
construction of tennis balls, he asked whether he

should ring them up. I abandoned my interest in his family, dropped all expectations of a lively exchange, and paid.

The first years here I felt on the lam. In the South a prerequisite for buying a bar of soap is the exchange of grandparents' names, their occupations, eccentricities, and favorite stories. Here, if they talked at all, clerks talked about the bar of soap. Cherishing anonymity themselves, they encouraged furtive behavior.

In those times a friend came to town without my phone number or address and thought to call the utility companies. Back home anyone who is asked a question instantly becomes a detective and devotes a week to cracking the case. Here the spokesman for the gas company said, "We're not talking, mister. Lot of folks here don't want to be found."

On the very day I learned the rules and skulked into a store, swaddled and with eyes averted and head bowed, I met a security guard and teen-age employees pointing and shouting, "Look at that old woman sneaking around in disguise! She's crazy. Guys, look at the crazy lady."

Since that moment the city has lacked not only my homey ways but also its frontier caution. Uniformly adolescent, clerks take as their only

58   business a closed social life within the store and, if they pay any mind at all, the glee they can find in the outsider as victim.

On a simple mission, I pursued an employee assiduously enough to buy an FM radio. The boy told me I'd have to take an AM-FM and condescended to let me look at the selection while he went to talk to Sam in another department. After half an hour he returned, still talking over his shoulder to Sam, and I said, "They all have clocks, those digital gizmos." "Sure they do. Which one do you want?" "I don't want a clock," I said, muttering that my idea of happiness is not knowing what time it is and not wearing shoes. "HEY, SAM! EVERYBODY, COME HERE! This lady don't wear SHOES. And she don't want a CLOCK." Sam offered, "Maybe she's doing TIME." After the hilarity waned, I settled for an AM-FM model with television bands, a weather channel, a thermometer, an auto plug-in (I don't want to know and didn't ask), and a clock now pasted over with tape.

Probably what made me break under the city-wide puberty regime was my fortieth birthday, the day after someone had nodded toward my exact contemporary and remarked to me, "I guess you're real proud of your daughter." On this birthday, which I hadn't thought to dread, I set out to buy a jar of face cream. The child in charge showed me a jigger of lotion and told me the price, a tithe of my monthly salary. I said, "This is good stuff. I've been using it for years, and I'm eighty-two." Looking at me for the first time, she studied my face and said, "You are? I don't think I would have known. GANG, COME HERE AND SEE THIS WOMAN. GUESS HER AGE!"

Since they are neither folksy parlors nor waystations for fugitives, local stores should institute the following rules:

1. No one under sixty-four will be hired.

2. Employees must not speak to one another in the presence of a customer.

3. When a customer approaches, the employee must terminate his personal telephone conversation.

4. If a customer wants to form a lasting friendship, the employee must seem to oblige.

5. If a customer wants anonymity and brevity, the employee must oblige.

6. Unless the customer initiates such behavior, employees may not attempt witticism or mockery.

7. If the customer jokes, the employee will laugh.

8. When a customer calls an employee by name, employee should check his name plate, and if he finds a match he should reply in a cordial manner.

9. If a customer appears with an item, cash in hand, a credit card, or a checkbook, the employee must feign interest.

10. Personnel must remove headphones and refrain from dancing while a customer is asking for attention.

The Horrible Diaper Joke

The Johnson Smith catalogue, its print smaller than the compact OED, sits before me with offerings as enticing as ever. With all the arrogance of an adult, I had thought it stopped publication about the time I reached legal maturity, but here it is. Neither of us has changed much.

As a child, I imagined a nationwide community of kindred souls who arranged life around Johnson Smith. Metropolitan children scrambled down flights of stairs to fetch the mail. Lone child after lone child stood bundled by RFD boxes through blizzards in northern plains states. Seafaring children sped to the nearest port. Thousands in towns like mine met the postman blocks away from home. Minds tuned to the

same compelling note, we studied the catalogue
by night and watched by day.

This latest edition has all the important
merchandise. Mixed in with newfangled
contraptions are the standard rubber-pointed
pencils, fake eggs, foaming sugar, dog messes,
whoopee cushions, hot candy, garlic gum, black
soap, shrunken heads ("the way the cannibals
prepared them"), and my old favorites, squirt
rings, spilled ink, disappearing ink ("If spilled on
tablecloth, handkerchief or clothes, it looks like
an ugly mess"), dribble glasses, and plate lifters.
Holding its own with solar gadgets and devices
from the space and computer age is the same
crystal set I assembled and listened to late at
night.

My dribble glass, lost during a move in
college, served dependably from grade school on.
Only today have I wondered what the matrons of
the neighborhood thought as, one by one on
successive days, they accepted the invitation of a
ten-year-old to come over for a drink. Each
visitor had two minutes of small talk before I
exclaimed, "My, but this is delicious water! Why,
I've almost finished mine, and you haven't even
begun." To a woman, they feigned chagrin when
water dripped onto the front of their print
dresses, and they laughed when the truth was

out. Through the years I routinely set the dribble glass at the guest's place for meals. It never failed. On page 51 in the new catalogue, it has kept its utilitarian design exactly.

The only Johnson Smith products that ever let me down were the midget camera, the ventriloquist's set, and the disguise kit. The camera, costing even now less than a roll of film, was a flimsy box with a crude aperture, and I could see through the seams. I had put more hope in Secrets of Ventriloquism because the ad promised, "Learn ventriloquism and apparently throw your voice. FOOL EVERYONE! Throw your voice into a suitcase, desk at school, another part of the room, dummy, animal, or anywhere. You'll get lots of fun fooling your teachers, parents, friends, etc." The set contained a little piece of cardboard with illustrated instructions on how to place it under the tongue. Instead of being able to project rude words to the schoolroom portrait of Mirabeau B. Lamar, I gagged on the sharp cardboard. If my dismay at the disguise kit was keen, the despair of my friend, now a monk, was agonized. We had hoped as fourth-graders suddenly to pass for adults and therefore get away with freewheeling mischief, as we can indeed do today. The kit gave him only a black paper moustache and some greasepaint. I wore

64   the greasepaint prophetically in a dentist's waiting
room to sit groaning with bruises painted over
my jaws.

People ordering from the catalogue have
reason for wild expectations. Bird Mess,
accompanied by a cartoon of a man in a straw hat
being dumped on by a deranged tweety-bird, is
touted as a "fantastically realistic plastic imitation.
Place anywhere. Harmlessly removed. Two
inches long. Nauseating." As a color photograph
shows, Crazy Bug-Out Eyes "create a laugh
riot. . . . A tilt of the head and they pop out,
another tilt and they pop back. Bloodshot color to
exaggerate the effect."

Johnson Smith rarely presents an item
carelessly without suggesting its suitable uses.
Lest the untutored reader believe for a minute
that Pocket Bird Call is only for calling birds, the
text adds, "great in classroom, library, church,
etc." Fake Spilled Coffee Cup becomes
"absolutely terrifying when placed on someone's
important papers," and Motorized Shark Fin is
for "your own pool or local beach." A literal mind
can find the stirrings of creative thought with
Glowing Monster: "Imagine the reaction of
friends or relatives if they were to awaken from
a sound sleep to see this monster advancing
toward them."

Coaxing, insinuation, and hints of success will

do for some items. Others call for demands and plain talk. Imitation Vomit, decorative though it may be, serves a greater purpose than that of a whatnot or objet d'art. "Place by baby, dog, dinner table or pretend you've been sick. Revolting." The wearer of Shoe Squeaker carries an obligation to "raise havoc in library, church, wedding." Johnson Smith stretches its patience with slow students in explaining Phony Squirt Catsup and Mustard containers: "When you 'squirt' at friends or relatives they'll think their clothes are ruined. . . . Every prankster should have both of these in his arsenal for special occasions."

Since Horrible Diaper Joke might seem to have limited possibilities to someone preoccupied with trivial concerns, the catalogue commands: "Leave on floor, hang on towel rack or put with load of clean laundry and watch the startled expressions." Bloody Mashed Rat, as if anyone could resist it, is "disgusting. Eleven-inch phony rubber rat [I guess it might be a real rubber rat] looks like it just got run over. Leave on kitchen or basement floor for real thrills. Use our No. 2180 Phony Blood for added effects."

Either truly gory products weren't in the catalogue in my heyday, or I was too squeamish to covet them. Joke Razor Blade I of course remember and may have owned. It "snaps on

66　finger" and "makes it look cut in half with plenty of blood." Probably a newcomer, Realistic Bloody Life-Size Joke Butchered Hand is a "full-size amazingly nauseating flesh-colored [a racist term, I've often thought] hand that appears to be freshly butchered at the wrist with blood oozing." I don't remember Horrible Accident Disguise Mask, which "fits over head and looks like you had a horrible accident," or the advice about where such attire is appropriate: "Wear while driving, sports, etc."

A devoted but lapsed Johnson Smith customer, I am glad to know that I have four of their offerings in my office right now: a pistol that releases a BANG flag, a squirt pen, a six-inch electric chair that shocks anyone who picks it up, and a clock that runs backward. None came from the great purveyors in Mt. Clemens, Michigan, but I'll stick with them now that I know they're still in business. Things change, however. The catalogue, called Johnson Smith's World of Fun, costs fifty cents, and the company accepts Visa and MasterCard. I'll try to fool them with Joke Vanishing Charge Cards. Watch your creditors squirm.

The Color of Your Parachute

Fashionable observers are talking more and more about job burnout and career changes in mid life. Since I seldom see anyone willingly leave a job he has managed to keep, I decided to do some prying. In the interests of research, I made myself privy to letters to an employment agency, a place likely to hear from people wanting a change in work.

The applicants in this sample do not mention mid life, though most seem to be thereabouts. Instead, they talk about the shifting times and a changing world, their inability to tolerate current conditions in their jobs, and a desire to use untapped talents. A few representative letters suffice to give menopause for thought.

68   Dear Good Samaritan Employment Agency:

I can't help noticing that your company's name has 29 letters.

My résumé looks as if I have jumped from job to job, but I have always had just one. I was a counter. Over the years I have ascertained the number of olives, artichoke hearts, pimientos, and nuts per jar, in jar after jar after jar. I have counted sheets of paper, aspirin, paper clips.

Having numbered in fact 2,306 different products in my career, I have turned completely away from counting and am directing my talents toward verbal accomplishment. Since my move from Krispy Kashew Kompany (19 letters), I have devoted two years and three days to my new endeavor, writing for magazines.

Quite frankly, I am disheartened by the 386 rejection slips I have received. For example, *Reader's Digest* returned "Marxism Makes Sense," "Nothing You Can Do Will Improve Your Health," "Optimism Is a Hoax," and my condensed version of *The Divine Comedy*.

All the popular women's magazines have turned down "No Marriage Should Be Saved," "Celebrities Opt for a Drab Christmas," "Throw Your Leftovers Away," "Princess Diana Tells Why Copying Her Designs Is Tacky and Reprehensible," "No One Wants a Homemade Gift," and "Decorating Idea—DON'T." *The New*

York Review of Books rejected "Health as Metaphor," "Barbara Cartland's Debt to Wittgenstein," "A Celebration of Our Vietnam Involvement," and "Tatum O'Neal Talks About Wrinkles."

Motor News sent back "Grand Prix Drivers prefer Mopeds," "Why Your Wife Should Choose Your Auto," "55 Is Too Fast," and "Making the Most With Retreads." *Field and Stream* rejected "Worm Fishing More Exacting than Fly-Fishing," "We Left Our Guns Behind and Played Whist," and "Bouillabaisse—A Grenade in the Pond Makes It Easy." *National Geographic* has ignored 34 of my articles, including "Gary, Indiana, Is Ugly," "Women of South Seas Prefer Olga Bras," and "Truly Boring Insects of Peru."

So, believing that a wise inconsistency is not the hobgoblin of big minds, I am prepared to abandon free-lance writing. Clearly one must have close personal contacts in the literary marketplace.

What I require of your company is a position with a publishing house or with any magazine. (*National Enquirer* rejected my "*Gödel, Escher, and Bach* Reconsidered," and *Cosmopolitan* has not even had the courtesy after 243 days to comment upon "Pig Farming: A Personal Account" or "Immanuel Kant's Test of Sexuality," but I would consider even them. After all, one

70   cannot expect sensibility or discernment or good
taste anywhere in a nation whose citizens
announce on television that they want to *be*
Oscar Meyer wieners and that they *are* peppers.)

I prefer to work alone, associating with as few
people as possible, but I do want to make use of
my way with words. My vocabulary reached
74,532 words at 2:07 today, and I expect it to
exceed 80,000 in 65 days.

Expecting to hear from you in 77 hours,

Basil McM.

Dear Employment,

Me and Bubba has worked rodeo's as a couple
for fifteen year's. Not that we have actual rode
for the last ten just doing other thangs at the
ground's. But at one time I was practicle Queen
of Barrel Racing and Bubba was regular all
around. So you can see we know Show Bidness
real good dont you.

Together we has broke about ever bone in the
human bidy but we are what youd call semi-
supple and can do the work of a dozen of the
younger folk's of today. We are not tahred
physicle just plumb wore and tuckered out so we
caint spit when spittin is call for by all them fancy
folk's what like to play like they know rodeoin
just because they have rode a imitation bull in

some yankee bar. We want to thow up when people what have never saw or did the real thang dres's up and brag and strut around like they was stuff dont you. Bubba swear's hed sooner run a horney toad farm than keep on mixin and manglin with the likes of them.

We want to work with the public and are thankin maybe of motel management. What do you thank.

Waneta and Bubba J.

Good Samaritan Employment Agency

Dear Agents:

I am interested in any opportunity you may have. For many years I have been an employee of a television show of Julia Child's, although after all this time I still do not honestly know whether that is her real name or her *nom de* spoon.

My chief responsibility has been to clean up the kitchen during and after the show. Neither my frustration tolerance nor my dexterity can be doubted. As the whisks drop, clogged with egg whites and chocolate, as the sticky bowls, pans, pots, and skillets are left mired in brandy, sugar, or gravy, the camera goes to a close-up of Child. Then I, crouched in a position no longer tenable for me, sneak onto the set and remove the

utensils quickly and silently. Not once have I
been seen or heard by the audience.

After the show my real work begins. That
kitchen is spotless entirely because of me. I have

demonstrated persistence and loyalty consistently. To be honest, once, during a particularly excruciating period of food flambé and boning birds, I composed a letter of resignation but never submitted it. Word may have gotten around, however, because for the week following Child actually replaced bottle tops and went so far as to schedule a meal using only twelve pans and twenty-six hand utensils. But the old routine resumed, and back I was with fowl drippings, scattered scallions, hollandaise splattered on every surface, counter tops like candied apples— much more.

An inspired cook, I'm sure, Child does not know the use of running water, the simple sponge, the trash basket, or the efficacy of using a knife or spoon more than once. I have served long enough. My ulcer rages at her cry of *'Bon appetit!'* "

Any employer will find me easy to work with, quiet, and eager to do my job. I believe in cleaning up as you go along and a place for everything and everything in its place.

If you have an opening even in Deep Fat, please consider me. Hours are of no importance, and I am willing to relocate, but I would prefer to be in a place where French is not spoken.

> Yours desperately,
> Kenneth S.

74 Agency,

For sixteen years since I was very, very young I have been the owner and only steady employee of Jump-Out-Of-A-Cake Entertainment International, Inc.

Until lately business at conventions and parties has been very active. I do put on a very impressive show, as these pictures definitely give an idea of. I am mailing you a list of some of the very large occasions I have been the center of which. These performances have been for many important personages. I could give you names.

My cake is definitely one of the very finest and largest in the world, and I ice it very expertly and very generously before every engagement. I am as vivid a jumper as can be found and a very good looker, smiler, and high-kicker. The talent is in the legs, and believe me I definitely keep in shape.

Something has definitely made business fall off very much all over the country, not just mine. Personages do not seem to want very fine entertainment of this nature any more. I do not know what they do instead.

Let me know if you have a place for a girl with my attributions. Maybe I can be an entertainer on television or in the movies or a tax accountant or definitely something in Congress.

Yours very truly
Starleen Le B.

The Color of Your Parachute

Dear Good Samaritan Employment Agency:

I am a mature man, a seasoned provider of oddments of information and astonishing facts used by newspapers as fillers. For years I enjoyed and took pride in my work. Some of my findings from the old days that crop up even now are, "If every common housefly lived to maturity, we'd soon be forty feet deep in common houseflies," and "If all the glaciers melted, New York would be under twenty-eight feet of water."

As times have changed, so has my business. The market is glutted with amateurish speculations such as a recent scrap that has been making the rounds: "If all the people in China jumped up and down on their seats at the same time, the United States would be engulfed by a tidal wave." You get my drift.

I believe we've reached our limits. We've already ascertained that the world has more photographs than bricks, more bricks than clocks, more clocks than hats. We can't get a line on a real zinger of an "if," the life-blood of creativity. Who cares what would happen if every llama in the world went to Memphis or if all the gallbladders removed in the last year were put in the Oval Office? If all the transistor radios in the country were turned on at once? They are. Forget dreaming up a good cataclysm.

We're not reaching the public. In the old days fillers caught the imagination. You could *feel* what

76   life would be like forty feet deep in common houseflies, but you can't put yourself in the Oval Office with gallbladders.

So I'm ready to go into another occupation. I'm a good team man and can bring experience, creativity, and good sense to a corporation or to public service. My career has suited me for a place in government, and I think this administration especially would appreciate a talent like mine.

Ed T.

In Freeze Drying Is the Preservation of the World

As a seasoned (salt, pepper, and plenty of thyme on my hands) camper, I must offer advice about taking to the woods. Around here a camper has two serious choices—state campgrounds and wilderness areas. Out of the question are KOA facilities, merely parking lots for movable motels, and the use of horses. The major characteristic of the horse (*equus caballus*, from, I imagine, *cabal*: plot, conspiracy) is its propensity for defying and injuring human beings. Some people claim to enjoy riding horses into the mountains, but I'd rather be aboard a pig, rhinoceros, or jackal.

Real camping is distinguished from what many of us do when we are traveling and recognize the symptoms of fatigue enough to stop and put a sleeping bag thirty feet from the road. The realer kind of camping leads to the wilderness. Any party of more than one includes an overly enthusiastic, highly experienced mountaineer who organizes the expedition. Typically, he presents to the group a map of the terrain with three trails charted. "Trail A," he says, "is worth the trip, interesting, and moderately challenging to the beginner. We'll see some wildlife. B is for tourists. Last year I hiked back down because in four days I saw two of them. Trail C I marked here as a private joke. It's for shut-ins." Always take Trail C. The shut-in route will challenge anyone who has yet to run barefoot up Mont Blanc.

Some of the disadvantages of hiking into a wilderness area to be alone with nature lie in "hiking," "wilderness area," "alone," and "nature."

"Hiking" means "to go with exertion of effort; to march laboriously." That's the pretty side. Hiking also entails wearing unattractive boots engineered to gnaw flesh, and carrying on the back a load of anvils, cargo that makes a body yearn to tote that barge and lift that bale.

Beautiful indeed, wilderness areas hold for the camper the charm of a pure world innocent of human development. What a life, we think, freedom from the tyranny of telephones, civilization, commerce. We can bathe in cool mountain streams, gape at the stars, listen to the pulse of the unadulterated world as it was meant to be and should always be. Mountain streams are not cool as hearsay would have us believe, but arctic. The stars provide wonderment for a few hours, but then a heavy heart realizes that they are not reading lamps. Freedom from telephone sacrifices the liberty to call a doctor at the onset of acute appendicitis and to summon information about the pulse of the unadulterated world: "If a flash of lightning precedes thunder by three seconds, how close is the bolt? Two seconds? One? Was setting this tent under the tallest tree a good idea?" The absence of commerce makes for headiness at our self-sufficiency and superiority to crass mercantilism—for a couple of days, just until the keen observer notes a lack of good restaurants. Freeze-dried carbohydrates sate fairly quickly, and, except for the purist who picks potentially lethal berries and likes to root around in the ground for edible vegetables (water hemlock is mighty like a parsnip, fool you every time— maybe taking a pig along isn't a silly notion: ham with truffles), the camper is stuck with boiling water at 10,000 feet for yet another serving of Library Paste Stroganoff.

A warning: Expect a man to be angry with a

80   woman who has watched patiently by the fire. He
is angry because he has experienced ecstasy in
some foolery like climbing a mountain face and
feels he has deprived her of such pleasure.
Women are smarter than men. That is why,
when fire and hearth were invented many years
ago, women volunteered to sit still to mind them.
The history of intelligence in this nation can be
traced by the popularity among women of shelling
peas, quilting, rocking babies, any excuse to sit
down.

Being alone tugs constantly as an ideal. What
we have in the back of our minds where
neurology begins to make sense is being at home
with books and records and old movies without
the drudgery of being at home. When we set out
for forests, we sing lustily, quote Hank Dave
Thoreau, and forget that being alone in the
wilderness means having no one, nothing to
blame and facing sticky issues such as our own
mortality. Household drudgery tags along nipping
at our raw heels. As everyone was thinking only
yesterday, again quoting Hank Dave, "Our life is
frittered away by detail. . . . Simplicity,
simplicity, simplicity! I say, let your affairs be as
two or three, and not a hundred or a thousand;
instead of a million count half a dozen, and keep
your accounts on your thumb nail." Numbering
into the hundreds, the pieces of gear carried into

the wilderness demand more fondling and complex attention than any equipment at home. Sailors at sea who swab and polish all day seem lazy and carefree in contrast to the camper who devotes daylight hours to cleaning, checking, and caressing every item.

Nature can be benevolent, malevolent, or indifferent, and we are wise to check in from time to time to see what kind of mood we are projecting onto her this season. (For "nature," see *King Lear.*) Nature includes the fragile columbine, the mighty peak, the graceful pine, the wistful willow, the friendly cow patty, the venomous rattlesnake, scorpion, and brown recluse. It excludes all domestic animals except dogs named Blue who wear bandanas around their necks and play frisbee in the wilderness. Being female, Nature has a way of getting back for some suspected wrong (who among us has not destroyed dandelions?) or for an imagined slight (who fully appreciated her last magnificent dust storm?)

The softy's alternative to a wilderness experience, as it is called, is state site car camping, which used to be convenient and pleasant. Nowadays the careful camper must realize that he will encounter Other People. Other People scream at each other. They scream all day long. They hop up long before a proper

82   hour and scream, "Day-vud! Day-vud! Come eat
your bay-kun." The birds hush their singing.
"Day-vud! Your bay-kun is getting cold!" After
Day-vud gets his whipping and the family's blood
sugar level rises, the group brays from high
spirits. "Pappaw, look! Everbidy looky here! A
prairie dog is setting by that old rotten fish we
thowed out. Bozette, get yoursef over to here
and see the little thang."

Other People come from all regions. At night a
couple certifiably Eastern argue maniacally: "I am
NOT saying that *Time* shouldn't be published!
You always distort. I am saying that—in terms of
morality, in terms of any aesthetic decency, in
terms of the terms in which I am speaking
existentially—people should not be allowed to
read *Time* in terms of itself."

The careful camper, bent on hearing the noises
of nature and on witnessing her spectacle, may
either admit that Other People are part of nature
or sleep at home in the yard or attend Audubon
Society meetings to watch movies of nature
unsullied and hospitable. When I want a whiff of
pure mountain air and a night under the canopy, I
usually sleep in the yard.

Next week, however, I'll give camping another
try in mountains I've never seen (Trail C). If that
doesn't work out, I'm chewing on an idea for
freeze-dried beer that will win a Nobel Prize and

make me rich, and then a helicopter can drop me into a pristine area with a generator to power a reading lamp and a far-reaching telephone with dial-out capability only and maybe a mute housekeeper, a mute cook, a mute doctor, and a mute dentist. A sedan chair is overstretching, but I think I'll take the pig.

Tell Us, Inc.

I am a good listener, too good. At leisure I fret about the ailments of distant relatives of strangers who have talked to me on public conveyances. Instead of solving global woes, I worry about poor Bertha and her bladder infection and wonder whether the sister of the man with the rhinestone tie ever found an apartment in West Covina. Nuclear waste accumulates while my attention goes to Kevin who, in setting out on a bus to find himself, lost his backpack.

Only recently did I realize that people don't remember what they have told me. Astonished looks and curses taught me not to rush up to anyone who in line long ago at a movie told me of plans or problems. I have stopped asking, "Did

86   you buy that four-wheel drive you wanted?"
because of the exchange that always follows:
"WHAT?" "You know, the car that would take you
to your cabin even in winter, the 'dandy vehicle,'
you kept calling it. And your family didn't want
you to get it because you'd just bought the chain
saw and the power tools and had turned the
basement into a workshop and your wife had just
found out that you'd been fooling around." "I've
never seen you before in my life, sister. Are you
the CIA or something?"

On any major corner in this country I could
recognize at least three people whose life stories
I know, people who should have suffered
laryngeal collapse and mandible exhaustion the
last time we met. Thinking as I do about
alternative careers, I propose a service industry
using my experience.

TELL US, INC. will hire out to listen. One of
our most elaborate productions is Tell Us Your
Trip. Clients may purchase only segments of the
program, but the full package includes our
hearing your initial account of travel brochures
with frequent calls for comparison and contrast of
destinations and accommodations followed by a
visit for your presentation of the final choice
accompanied by all reasons and benefits. We will
hear readings from guide books, descriptions of
clothing, accessories, gadgets, and luggage, and

88 portrayals of travel agents and their vagaries. Our lines are open all night to receive anxieties about whether you should take the lining to your all-weather coat. On your return we assemble groups of trained listeners for marathon slide shows and for the viewing of souvenirs. We want to know the conditions surrounding the snapping of each photograph, the provenance of each curio, and descriptions of every clerk, driver, and innkeeper. Our listeners cry out for the details of every lost object, of every rude encounter, of every delay and inconvenience.

For a flat fee we offer standard services: Tell Us Your Operation, Tell Us Your Diet, Tell Us Your Philosophy of Life. For the same charge we will hear about your pets, the glories or sorrows of your kin, the causes of your success or failure, your reasons for not taking self-improvement courses.

More costly is our attention to your narratives about marital difficulties or the reasons you didn't buy real estate when it was cheap. No amount of money is enough to procure our ear for everyday complaints, stories of slights, or speculations about the motives or private lives of others.

Tell Us Your Political Views works on an escalating scale, with a modest charge for liberals (including rental of the Plumbers Hall) and a big chunk for reactionaries (not including the steak dinner the speaker buys for us). We provide bunting, hecklers if desired, applause, and television coverage.

Plans for TELL US, INC. are still on the drafting table, but immediately available is my telephone service, Tell Me Why You Feel Guilty.

Caint Glow for Perspirin

People around me have been making pointed references to a new article by an authority on speech who announces that the voice is the window to the soul (garbled Plato, and I like mine Kristeller clear). This guru can twist larynxes and tongues to conform to a standard, which my auditors clearly would prefer.

True, I have noticed problems in talking and have developed formulaic answers. Several times a week I answer the phone to hear the caller ask, "Is your mommy or daddy at home?" I give my parents' area code and number and try to work in big words. Old friends complain, "You speak so softly that we've never heard half of what you've said." "That's why we're still friends." Strangers demand, "Where did you get

92   that accent?" "The Loretta Lynn School of Elocution."

Surely many of us have high, soft voices and show a geographic determinism in our speech. These distinguishing characteristics shouldn't cripple us so.

The top register makes us unable to sound authoritative or grown-up. We can't fulminate, and fulminating seems like great fun for the fulminator. Occasionally I lower my voice in calls to unreasonable creditors or in interrupting obscene phone messages. One night I successfully shooed away a burglar by booming, "Halt! You are surrounded." These efforts are only momentary since I don't knowingly consort with creditors, obscene callers, or burglars.

Soft speech, while allowing us to get away with a lot, makes the deepest conviction sound like an aside to the wind. This society crazily values audibility. A soft voice hampers the training of pets, though not, I sincerely believe, of children or adults. It doesn't help in telling umpires and players what to do during a game. It too crimps fulmination. Getting away with a lot, however, outweighs almost all the disadvantages. I can always say in truth, "This is nothing I wouldn't tell him to his face."

A regional accent, if it happens to be maverick, undercuts credibility but provides amusement to those who think freaks are funny. I receive long-distance calls asking me to talk to a sequence of party-goers in the Midwest, California, or New York. If I can enhance their revels, wonderful.

A regional peculiarity is the greatest nuisance of all, but not from being misunderstood. Everyone feels misunderstood nowadays, and at least I don't take it personally. That people often take dialect for inability to handle the language bothers me. Someone who has grown up speaking French, Spanish, or Italian is admired for his fluency in English. But a quarter of this nation of native speakers is made to feel that English is a second or third language, so we are left without a first language. At the Metropolitan Museum I carried on an animated conversation with a man who seemed intelligent and informed, as I thought I did, holding up my end just fine. As we parted, he asked, "And what language do you speak in your country?"

Those who change their speech to disguise their origins or to blend in with new communities are throwing away part of their identity—on purpose. Anyone who doesn't talk like others back at the home place has worked at homogenizing his speech in maturity. A change doesn't come from unconscious assimilation, nor does childhood instruction make a difference.

My sister remembers our father, a Nova

94 Scotian, trying to teach her to get the Texan out of her pronunciation, but by the time I came along he had given up. Recently, on a visit home for both of us, my sister and I collided at the announcement desk of a shopping emporium, each assuming the other had wrested control of the microphone. We hadn't heard that accent except from each other for years.

Speaking from the soil that nourished us seems right to do. Our natural registers and volumes mark us as individuals, each as different from another as a horny toad and an armadillo on a night so dark you caint see cow patties and so hot you caint glow for perspirin and caint perspire for sweatin and caint spit for cussin.

I would no more consider changing the way I speak than my politics, system of ethics, diurnal rhythms, friends, family. And you can bet your last sowbelly durned dollar I'm not fixin to take lessons in talkin if it means dippin into my face-lift fund.

Is This the Party to Whom I Am Speaking?

Most of us go through stages in dealing with solicitors. I've been brusque, inconvenienced, snippy, legalistic, obligingly difficult, tedious, and submissive. Now I believe I've gone over the edge.

The brusque mode left me unsatisfied, so I tried lecturing on the insensitivity, rudeness, and immorality of interrupting me, especially since I had made a point of seeing that my number is unpublished. (I have a real flair for keeping things unpublished.) I made up fanciful stories about how busy I was. As much as these autobiographical fictions amused me, the caller was unmoved. She knew when she took the job that interruption was the game, that no one is

96   idle enough to stare longingly at a phone willing it
to ring so that a stranger can deliver an
exposition of introductory rates for steam-
cleaning carpets. She also knew the likelihood of
my having answered while performing emergency
neurosurgery prefatory to setting out on a
concert tour of Brazil.

Snippiness made me feel petty the rest of the
day, and legalism, transparent and tawdry, failed:
"Give me your full name, the name of the alleged
company you purport to represent, its listing
number with the Corporation Commission, its
address, and the names of the principal owners.
Soliciting by telephone is expressly forbidden by
clause 429G of code 3450, section 812,
addendum 48."

My favorite ploy would have charmed me had I
been the caller, but solicitors are single-minded in
their quest for a sale. When offered a full-color 8
× 10 studio portrait of my family and me, four 5
× 7 prints, and, as a bonus for acting now, 10
free wallet-sized color prints, I would ask, "Do
you photograph pets?" "Why, yes, Madam!
You're in luck. If you'll bring them in before noon
on Thursday, we'll be glad to make a full-color 8
× 12 studio portrait of your pets." "Wonderful.
May I come at 10:30 Thursday then? But wait.
How long will the sitting take?" "Probably half-an-

hour or an hour." "Oh, too bad. You see, my pets passed on some time back, and I keep them in the freezer in individual custom-made Tupperware containers, and I'm afraid they'd thaw." The woman on the other end of the line was, I knew, scratching my name off a list and rehearsing her speech for the next victim.

Then I tried being sweetly difficult. "Let me see. Your question is whether I am the lady of the house. My mother taught me all those distinctions, and I'm reasonably certain that generally I'm honorable, courteous, and clear-eyed. But right now the house is a mess—I'd be ashamed for you to see it. Excuse me, what is your name? Well, Pam, no lady would let things go the way I have. 'Deferred maintenance' is what realtors generously call the kind of rubble I've allowed. To tell the truth, Pam, over the years I've deferred maintenance to my own person by avoiding exercise, neglecting to balance the basic food groups, refusing to shop for clothes—Isn't shopping a bore? And the prices! Only last month I saw a fetching little cotton shift in a store window, but, Pam, you wouldn't believe me for a minute if I told you the price—and pretty much just letting myself go, though I do floss every day, and I hope you do too, Pam, because dental hygiene now when

98 you're young, and you sound young, prevents
pain and expense later on and doesn't take much
time since you can floss while you read or watch
television, as if anything good were ever on
television except *NBC News Overnight*—Oh,
Pam, I hope you watch that, but no, of course
you can't since you are up so very early to make
your calls. Why, it's not quite daylight, is it?
Pam, let me reach for some orange juice, and
we'll get back to your question."

During my next phase—submission—I bought
a book of coupons worth thousands of dollars. To
whom the thousands accrue the caller did not
make clear, but the bargains are staggering: one
free battery with paid purchase of complete home
sound system; one free emery board with
purchase of facial, manicure, make-up
consultation, haircut, tinting or frosting,
permanent, and wig, wiglet, or fall; alignment
absolutely free with purchase of four new tires;
one beverage free with purchase of four family-
style meals at the Masai Red Milk Diner.

In December a man rang the doorbell and
asked whether he could cut down one of my
trees. "Yes," I said. "Which one?" he asked. "You
choose." A rich yuletide camaraderie grew among
him and the man spreading steer manure and the
man patching stucco and the man installing a

solar contraption and the boy rearranging grit on
the windows and the man delivering load after
load of life-time light bulbs, the pesticide crew,
the preventive plumbers who clear lines *before*
they become a problem, the man who removed
unsightly stains and blemishes from the driveway,
and the teenager hired as handyman who had yet
to find his talent and whiled away the season on
my porch working on his bicycle.

   I am not a rich woman, not even a solvent
one. So despite the pleasure of saying yes to
everyone I had to change my ways with
solicitors. Although retribution rarely works,
especially the scatter-fire brand I think up, now I
practice a contrary, deflected vengeance. It
began, naturally, with the telephone, when I
called dance studios and told them that they had
been selected at random to win the opportunity,
if they acted promptly, to offer me five free
dance lessons. I called radio stations and said I
would give them all my money if they could
guess the exact amount. Then I moved on to
calling banks, asking for an officer, and
announcing that I had a question concerning
American history which if answered correctly
within thirty seconds would entitle him to grant
me a loan, absolutely interest free.

   Expansion often leads to lunacy, and now I go

100   from door to door. "Hello," I say. "I'm Mary
       Bess, and I wonder whether you could sell me a
       Watchtower. Or maybe you have some Avon
       products for sale. I'm interested in aluminum
       siding for my house. Sometimes I worry that my
       life insurance is not adequate to protect my
       family."

A Mavis Foster Day

The fashion of saying "Have a good day" offends many people. Not me. It beats, "Lady, that'll be 254 dollars." (When anyone calls me "Lady," the bill is always over 100 dollars.)

A sign of general well-wishing, "Have a good day" differs from "Good-bye," a contraction of "God be with ye," in its failure to invoke divinity and in setting a time limit on the blessing. That we have turned our prayers from sustained benediction to an imperative for a single good day shows a shift in our collective dread. As a nation we have left behind fears of spiritual decay, personal combat with Satan, and dire physical events such as death and mutilation to worry instead about what must have seemed negligible in earlier times—a bad day.

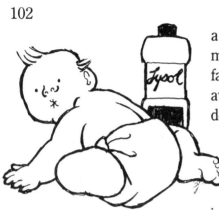

A bad day comes from a confluence of minor mishaps, mechanical failures, intentions gone awry, surly remarks, dental appointments, intractable corporate policies, demands, tiny erosions of time. The events in themselves have little importance, but they accumulate quickly and unrelentingly, each new one nettling to the fourth power of the one before.

One of the problems with a bad day is that it can't be claimed. We need a system of recognition and support for the victim. Friends, church members, colleagues, and neighbors should bring hams, flowers, and casseroles. Offices should close early in observance. (At

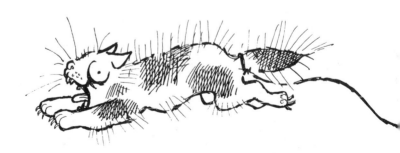

least one of the misadventures usually stems
from a closed office, but the victim of a bad day
needs public condolence all the same.)

Broadcasters should
interrupt their
schedules to
announce:
"An update
on Mavis
Foster's bad
day. Her son
is still
barricaded in
the basement
with the kittens
and fireworks. Her

daughter maintains silence about whether she
drank the Lysol or fed it to the baby. The
mechanic has issued a revised statement to the
press that her car needs new wiring as well as a

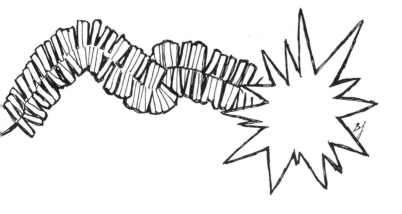

new alternator. On this, her holiday, the office
called with eight urgent messages and the news
that a young man known as Dopey Dewey has
been promoted over her. A friend she barely
remembers from high school has just phoned to
say that he and his family are in town and can
stay with her for several days. This just in! As
Mavis Foster stood in line to pay postage due on
a letter, the strap on her new purse broke and
the car she had borrowed received a parking
ticket. Electricity is now off in her block. Stay
tuned for information on the situation as it
develops. Our minicam crew is at the scene and
will have a full report at six. Again—DAY
WORSENS FOR MAVIS FOSTER!"

A bad day is no time to ponder world famine or
the possibilities of nuclear devastation. Altruism
and concern for one's fellow man should go out
the window with the bathwater *and* the baby.
The victim may, with clean conscience, turn to
an insulation of self and contemplate the seeping
away of spirit and volition. The old saying about

being sad at having no shoes until meeting a man   105
who has no feet ignores (1) human nature, (2)
the inherent inability of apodalness to give cheer,
and (3) the right of the individual to sinking
solipsism, a retreat from the progression of a bad
day. We have an inalienable right, on a bad day,
to the pursuit of wooden despair and self-pity just
as surely as we have the right to scamper after
happiness on a good day.

"A SPECIAL BULLETIN: Mavis Foster's neighbor
is resting well in a local hospital after injuries
sustained as she said, 'Mavis, honey, cheer up.
You'll look back on all this and laugh.' "

The Whole Confusion and Nothing But

I've been hearing some high-flown and scary talk about the moral and legal accountability of advisers. The question seems to center on who is responsible if someone acting on advice commits an act that leads to injury. Accepting a degree of moral responsibility makes sense, especially if it means feeling guilty, but *legal* accountability?

I see myself on the witness stand in a navy dress with a crisp white collar. "Ms. Whittling, how well do you know the defendant?" "We're friends." "Can you be more specific?" "We've known each other for six years, and we talk on the phone once or twice a week and give each other birthday and Christmas presents." "Ms. Whiffle, are you in the habit of advising the

108 accused?" "We exchange advice sometimes. She's good at practical matters, and I—well, I guess I can help her with the impractical, I mean nonpractical, or a-practical areas, matters that don't have to do with finances or cooking."

"Thank you Ms. Whitford, for giving the jury this fine evidence of your stability. [*Chuckle.*] Now please tell the court what you said to your alleged friend, the defendant, on April 2." "I wished her success at her job interview and told her I knew she'd make a good impression." "Ms. Whitterly, what were your exact words to the defendant?" "I don't remember. I probably said, 'Good luck. You'll do fine.' " "Did you advise her to take a specific action?" "I don't believe I did."

"Ms. Whippet, are you aware of the events of April 3 in the personnel office of Zeugma Corporation? Do you know that eight people lie in hospitals with injuries from the events of April 3 and that the defendant, your alleged friend, sits before us today with her leg in a cast?" "Yes."

"Think back to your conversation with the defendant on the eve of that spectacle so bizarre that it has attracted worldwide attention. What did you say?" "I've told you everything I can remember." "We have heard testimony from the defendant that you advised her to bowl them over. Did you use those words?" "If I did, I didn't mean them literally." "Then you may have used those words?" "Maybe, but I never dreamed. . . ." "The defendant has testified under oath that you instructed her to knock them cold and then to break her own leg. Did you, Ms. Whistle, give such perverse counsel to your alleged friend?"

My collar by now is no longer crisp, and I blurt, "Look, I know Mavis has her nose out of joint and wants to come out of this mess smelling like a rose, but that evening she was really excited, on cloud nine, high as a kite. In some ways she's still wet behind the ears, born yesterday, a little rough around the edges, but when she modeled her interview suit she had just stepped out of a band box, and she was dressed to the nines, beaming to beat the band, grinning from ear to ear. She was scared, though, because she didn't know whether she'd be interviewed by a tiger or a lamb or a social lion or a mouse or a fox or a rat. I just wanted to put a spring in her step.

"I honestly don't remember whether I told her to bowl them over and knock them cold and break a leg. I might have suggested that she elbow her way in, make a dent, bend an ear, steamroll through, put her foot down, step on some toes, tackle the problem, wrestle it to the ground, kick it around, corner it, chase it down, dissect it, sink her teeth into it, rip it apart, can

110   it (Mavis makes wonderful preserves every
year), bury it under, hit below the belt, chew
them up, tear them apart, take their breath
away, mow them down. . . ."

"ORDER! Court is recessed until Ms. Whittier
can bite her tongue—uh, until she can be
quieted."

Tongue in Buttonhook

For years I have been mystified by directives that come to me saying, "We don't want any broken field runners," "We need a utility infielder," or "Punt if you have to."

Sports signify to me an occasion to celebrate the seasons. I enjoy the lethargy of baseball and the aggressive nip of football and the fetid coziness of basketball. Since I've rarely watched games on television to hear the "color commentary," I'm ignorant of the vocabulary.

In order to do my work I must understand memos that come my way, and surely others as innocent as I am must have a problem deciphering the metaphors of sports. Someday communiqués will depend on accurate readings of words such as *bodice, Cimabue, parboil, Mildred*

112 *Pierce, synecdoche, hemstitch, arpeggio, blanch,*
and *appliqué,* but until such happy time here is a
glossary of game terms that spill over into real
speech. For handy reference I indicate
parenthetically the fields from which they in turn
derive.

buttonhook—the pattern made by a player who
runs one direction for a ball and then the other
direction (sewing)

blitz—a linebacker's rush (military)

hit for a cycle—make a single, double, triple,
and a home run in one game (laundry)

taking the collar—not getting a hit (the clergy)

post pattern—the running of a player down the
field and then crossing it (philately and sewing)

Hail Mary—a situation in which time is running
out and the halfback has lost the ball and hopes
somebody catches it (religion)

xyz—receivers in football (the world of letters)

dribble—a bouncing of the ball (child care)

air ball—a thrown basketball that touches nothing (medieval science, the other balls being fire, earth, and water)

bring iron—to hit the rim in basketball (metallurgy)

bad hands—the inability to catch a ball (theology and anatomy)

shock troops—substitutes in football (military)

Four Horsemen—backfield for Notre Dame (apocalyptic literature)

double-dipper—two games played by the same teams in a single day (culinary arts)

hitting a rope—hitting a line drive (hangman's lore)

swinging from the heels—hitting at the ball with great effort and missing (Watergate)

playing above the rim—hands above the basket (Grand Canyon)

mudder—one who plays well in inclement weather (agriculture and maternity care)

114   *full count*—the situation of having three balls
and two outs (history of imbibing among
European nobility)

hat trick—the making of three goals in one
hockey game (prestidigitation)

body check—slamming a player against the wall
(medical)

face-off—a situation in which two hockey
players have the puck between their sticks
(leprosy)

Mr. October—Reggie Jackson (the Julian
calendar)

hooker—one who makes the ball go to the left
or in a direction opposite to the throwing arm or
to the side of the ball on which it was struck
(angling, with possible reference also to *The
Laws of Ecclesiastical Politie,* 1594 and 1597, by
Richard Hooker)

banjo hitter—player with no power (American
Folk music)

sacrifice fly—a high ball hit by a player so that
another can score (military, especially the

suicide play—a situation in which the runner starts for home plate and the batter taps the ball gently (*Hamlet*)

monster—defensive back in football (classical mythology)

wheels—legs (vehicular locomotion)

How 'bout them dogs!—something people say in Georgia (veterinary science)

Crab Apples

Every autumn I grow indefatigably sentimental.
I don't do anything so creative as arranging
gourds, colored ears of corn, or ristras, but I
throw myself into the spirit of Harvest Home and
Thanksgiving.

To celebrate the season I survey yellow
cottonwoods along the Rio Grande, gape at
aspens, and garner as many Corrales vegetables
as I can manage. Humming "We Gather
Together," I shuck corn, shell black-eyed peas,
and roast green chile.

The height of my annual ceremonies in praise
of the earth's plenty is a pilgrimage to Agnew's
apple farm, widely and justly admired for its
apples and location. The drive from Albuquerque
through Pueblo land shows mesas, mountains,

and valleys, and the orchard itself testifies to the miracle of fecundity on the high desert.

The Agnews themselves are beloved and romanticized by people in these parts. Last week a friend, idly speculating, asked, "What do you think they do in the winter?" I knew the answer. "They sit by the fire and plan their attack on me." They must.

Each fall I deceive myself that at the end of the road I'll find my private vision of them: Mrs. Agnew smiling, plump, russet-cheeked, wiping her hands on her apron before she gives a hug of welcome, and Farmer Agnew hooking his thumbs into the straps of his overall bib as he drawls, "Shucks, Ma'am, we're mighty proud that you went to all thet trouble of comin' here for a visit."

Instead they stand slim and silent, poised in their L. L. Bean parkas, in wait for combat. Something about me sets them off, and I shouldn't be surprised. The Swiss as a nation hate me and swat at me for infractions of rules I don't know. Within minutes I enrage every clerk in any shop with "Alpine" in its name by my posture, odd interests, lack of industry, inattention to detail, and indifference to strict routine. The enmity of Switzerland doesn't bother or puzzle me, but every year I imagine that I can buy apples in my homeland without causing a fight.

Crab Apples

This fall I rolled all my sweetness up into one ball and tossed it gently to the Agnews. "For several years," I said with sunny gratitude, "you have been kind enough to sell me a few boxes of your splendid apples for me to send to my mother and father. They are looking forward to another shipment, and, my, aren't these apples especially beautiful!" Beaming, I stood modestly to receive their blessings and kind words.

Outraged, Mrs. Agnew flew to battle: "BOXES? NO BOXES! We have never given anyone a box! NEVER! You have never had one of our boxes! NEVER!" Unaware, once again I had touched a nerve. With cunning, the Agnews had also touched a nerve. "Please forgive me," I said, "but someone who looks just like you has sold me boxes of apples for many years." *"We are the Agnews,"* Farmer Agnew proclaimed. "Well, I'm pleased as cider to know you," I said, "and, if you'll permit, I'll just shuffle down here and pick up some of these heavy bags of apples and take them home and try to find a box to ship them in." *"You can't have a box. We don't give boxes to anyone. If* anybody here has ever let you have a box, it was an unauthorized act. *We are the Agnews!"*

"No *if* about it, Mr.—I didn't catch your name. Year after year I leave here with boxes of apples." Four Agnew eyes narrowed, revealing many months of practice at venomous glares with the aid of videotapes and a scowl coach. In unison, they said, "You

have never had a box from here. *No boxes!*"

As they trembled with righteous fury, I moseyed through the aisles, the spirit of Harvest Home dashed and my appreciation of apples red and yellow faded to Lucky Strike Green gone to war. I returned to face New Mexico Gothic. "If," I proposed, "I bought some of those handsome boxes of apples with 'Agnew' written all over them, would you empty them and give me only the apples? Or could I walk out of here with boxes with apples in them?"

"You can buy boxes of apples."

"May I, please? That's all I've ever asked."

"You asked us to *give* you a box. We don't give away boxes."

"May I buy a box of apples?"

"We don't sell boxes."

"If I buy a box filled with apples, do I get the box?"

"Why, of course."

My celebration of harvest complete, I turn to being thankful. Last year I was especially grateful for church bells that rang every quarter-hour, reminding me of great cultural centers such as Paris, London, Rome, Austin. I called the church to give thanks, but the woman who answered didn't know the church had bells, though I could hear them chiming over the phone as we talked. I have written stores to thank them for their courtesy through the year and have received replies saying that if I would come into the store and make my complaint directly to the manager the problem could probably be resolved to my satisfaction.

I persist in the belief that autumn is a time for rejoicing in our harvest and for giving thanks. My attempts are clumsy, easily misconstrued, but sincere. I want to thank the State of New Mexico for opportunity, humor, and friendship. Don't get me wrong.

Pleased to Be Invited

Those less serious of mind than I am have been frittering away their time maligning cocktail parties. These critics refuse to consider as entertainment anything which doesn't put chairs under their bottoms and entrées under their belts. Whether they are simply hungry and tired, they pose the metaphysical questions, "Who enjoys cocktail parties?" and "What kind of imbecile can stand them?"

The answer, and I am the one near the back waving my hand, is that I love cocktail parties. Although I don't drink cocktails—and therein may lie a clue—I commend to carpers the food, structure, and opportunity.

The food is never bad. Hosts who can't or

124 won't put in time preparing a finely orchestrated dinner can usually lay out interesting grazing materials. The best parts of life are the appetizers.

The structure of a cocktail party allows each person dozens of exit lines. A dinner party has a limit of one per person, and the allotted time arrives long after the proper context. A cocktail party permits frequent parting strokes as the exiter rushes off in search of "more of this exquisite squid and fig pâté in little cream puffs." Seated at dinner next to Pomposity itself, one can issue only little parries and hope the time for their giant culmination won't come, just this once, Lord, this once, when everyone is putting on a coat and telling the hosts goodbye. At sit-down events, as in life, Pomposity usually wins.

As youngsters we were told that at parties we should mix and mingle. For years in Texas I thought we had the polite necessity to mix and *mangle,* but the difference in most circles lay in pronunciation. I enjoy mixing, mingling, and mangling when mangling is called for. No arena sets up Pomposity for repeated mangling more handily than a cocktail party. After suffering only a few minutes of obsessive arrogance, the mangler can utter with perfect timing the exit line to end all exit lines and can exit swiftly to return to deliver yet another when it pops into mind. Listening from behind a fica, the alert deflater can zip by Pomposity's group with a sally on the way to guacamole.

At these parties old friends can exchange affection and fabric-of-life essentials without having either to tell all or hear details. Few items of gossip are worth much time, though we need to keep up on events. A cocktail party allows for transfer of tidbits without tedious ploddings into motive, speculations of outcome, and outpourings of feelings of the teller who has suffered through a dissimilar situation. When someone says, "Hubert has left Maude and has taken up with a younger woman," you say, "Oh, how dreadful! Let's have lunch," and hasten to greet anyone across the room.

Once or twice a year comes a piece of gossip deserving background information, sustained narrative, analysis, and conjecture. "Mavis took all the gerbils to New York and released them in the Museum of Modern Art. Before she left she burned all of Harold's *National Geographics,* and today he got a postcard from St. Tropez saying, 'Don't worry about a thing. You and the children will be well provided for.'" You say, "Why don't we wander into the laundry room a minute so you can tell me a little more?" You might not

126   have run into this informant for months, and at a
dinner party he might have felt constraint about
spilling the goods, especially if a guest of honor,
a visiting dignitary, were present.

Guests of honor can be a delight or a pain. A
cocktail party gives several opportunities to make
a determination because of the constant need to
see that everyone within hailing distance has food
and drink. When, or if, topics change, you can
sample the conversation the way you're sampling
the food and leave the group, give it another
chance, or decide to stay for a while.

The purest example of equal opportunity in the
world, a cocktail party lets everyone circle every
sphere (a complex geometric metaphor I often
use at parties to excuse myself on the grounds of
fatigue and disorientation) and join or reject.
When you see a group intent upon exploring a
subject, you can slither up and listen
inconspicuously until you find the topic to be
parity, treatments for tennis elbow, recipes for
cauliflower pudding, ideas for reorganizing a
company to maximize while optimizing, and you
can be off in a flash to check the cheese tray. If
you are in the mood for progressive puns and
another cares at the moment only for the
comparative qualities of snow tires and chains or
the problems of marked funding, he can wander
to more congenial company.

Those who scorn the cocktail party as superficial, noisy, and boring might consider what real life has to offer. Both are a lot of fun, and I'm pleased to be invited.

'Twas Brillig in the Soup du Jour

I am not a memorizer of poetry—or of much
else besides the alphabet, the multiplication
tables through eleven, and my mother's recipe
for pecan pie. If called on to recite, I could
stammer the beginning of "The Night Before
Christmas," supply the first line of a few sonnets,
and garble parts of "Jabberwocky." I even mess
up "Thirty days hath September," thinking not of
numbers but of which months have an *r*. Verse
mnemonic devices never work for me. Twice a
year I remind time-conscious friends to "spring
back, fall forward," a good rule of life anyway.

Poetry pops into my mind only without
summons, and since I blurt it out in a context
known only to me, my hearer is baffled or
offended. "What a pretty yellow dress you're

wearing," says a kindly soul. My gracious reply is, "All seems infected that th'infected spy,/As all looks yellow to the jaundic'd eye." In a grocery store I usually sneeze between the rows of detergents, and someone says, "Bless you." In my most despairing Macbeth choke, I lament, "I had most need of blessing, and 'Amen'/Stuck in my throat." When anyone asks if I know the time, I hear myself emoting: "The time is out of joint—O cursed spite,/That ever I was born to set it right!"

Rarely is verse appreciated except on greeting cards. I have a friend who did a brief stint as temporary office help. On a new assignment with a brokerage firm, she arrived as everyone else went to a meeting, leaving her to answer the phone. The first caller demanded, "Give me a quote." She said, "Tomorrow, and tomorrow, and tomorrow,/Creeps in this petty pace from day to day/To the last syllable of recorded time. . . ." The man on the other end of the line told her exactly what to do with her tomorrows.

Since I believe I don't remember poetry, the metrics that push forward to my mind and therefore my mouth always surprise and delight me, though others don't share the pleasures. Scenery elicits whole stanzas. Mountains are a snap, and I can usually reproduce fragments of

Byron, Shelley, and Keats, and swing into "Hills
peep o'er hills, and Alps on Alps arise" before
being gagged by those nearest and dearest. The
fiercest attack on these spontaneous eruptions
came at the beach. I had offered snippets of
Shakespeare, some Coleridge, the whole of
"Dover Beach," and was just launching into
Tennyson when a crowd of strangers circled
around, menaced with their Boogie boards, and
shouted as one, "Stop! Stop! Stop!" I bear a scar
on my left temple from a hurled Coppertone
bottle.

Mountains, oceans, the seasons, forests,
rivers, cities, villages—all conjure iambic lines.
But last week at the Grand Canyon my resources
failed. On the trip there I'd used up my desert
pieces, even "Ozymandias," and as I stood on the
rim the only poem to crop up was "Erosion."
After waiting a few minutes hoping something
better would come, I heard myself declaim:

> Little drops of water
> And little grains of sand
> Run along together
> To destroy the land.

As soon as the other tourists began consulting
one another about commitment procedures in

132 Arizona, I ducked into the bar at El Tovar and said, "So set 'em up, Joe; I've got a little story you ought to know."

Joe looked tolerant and benign, as bartenders are trained to look, so when he brought my order I continued: "I have forgot much, Cynara! gone with the wind,/Flung roses, roses riotously with the throng. . . ./I cried for madder music and for stronger wine. . . ." Poems spewed forth, poems I didn't know I knew, poems about taverns, ale, grog, possets, rum. I was on a roll.

During my recitation another patron pushed a speared, evil pot plant between us to muffle the meter and to signal that poetry was not the mode of the day. Instantly I quoted couplets I had last thought of in high school when a friend submitted them as a joke to a local poetry contest. [He won.]

> Ah, polytentacled specter avert,
> Flourishing in an urn of dirt!
>
> Thou hast exhumed in me
> The ghost of fiery poesy!

Joe, my former ally, came to me and snarled, "That'll be $1.50 for the Dr. Pepper. Go look at the Canyon." Drawing on the sympathy bartenders distribute with drinks, I leaned forward. "The canyon is the one thing I can't look at, Joe. Nothing comes to mind but 'Erosion.' " "My name's not Joe, lady, and it's sure not Cynara. It's Percy Bysshe Blunt. That Dr. Pepper's on the house if you'll go away right now."

It's not easy living day to day knowing I've let down the Grand Canyon.

True or False

Periodicals on the stands at grocery stores are turning serious. This season, wedged between "What Your Toothpaste Tube Reveals About Your Personality" and "How to Bring Romance Back [*back?*] to Laundry," is "Are You an Alcoholic?" The severity of this test differs from magazine to magazine. Here are two representative examples.

Test A: Answer each of the following True or False. Be honest.

1. Occasionally I say that a meal without wine is like a day without sunshine.

2. Frequently I choose baba au rhum over lime jello with marshmallows.

3. After working many hours in the sun I often

136   imagine that a cold beer might be refreshing.

4. At the end of an unusually bad day I sometimes think that I could use a drink with friends to unwind.

If you answered True to *one* of these, you are an alcoholic and need immediate treatment.

Test B: Answer True or False to each statement.

1. If I were offered an all-expenses-paid stay anywhere in the world for a month on the condition that I not drink before noon, I would refuse to go.

2. In the past week I have been asked to leave a public place for gnawing on the Naugahyde furniture.

3. In my bedroom I often see a Tasmanian devil riding a hyena through a pool of sorghum molasses.

4. I do not remember the last three months.

If you answered True to *all four* statements, you may have a drinking problem. The next time your physician comes into the bar you might mention it.

Alcoholism is deadly and should indeed be spotted and treated, but these tests have as much to do with an alcoholic as litmus paper has in determining the quality of a soufflé. Their real uses are clear. *Test A:* Gerald straightens the magazine on his lap and announces crisply, "Margaret, this confirms what I've suspected. You are an alcoholic. That explains those piña coladas at the Jamesons last summer. I am committing you to an institution." *Test B:* Harry stumbles out of bed crying, "Maudie, Maudie, good news! I'm not a drunk! I answered True just twice. Not a drunk. Call whatshisname, you know, my boss. Not a drunk." Maudie hugs him and says, "Honey, you're reading! That's wonderful."

You may already be devising little tests of your own for use in the home or office. Any supervisor will recognize your value when you show her/him your perfect score on "Are You a Compulsive Worker?"

1. I often finish my work only a few weeks after the deadline.

2. I realize that when a task is boring it should be left undone.

3. Sometimes I arrive at meetings before they are adjourned.

4. Goals, criticism, details, and demands slow my pace. If you are yourself a supervisor or employer, doubtless you have been administering your own quirky version for years.

138   At home you might want to gather your brood and intone, "Here is something of interest to all of us, a test. Let me read it to you, and we'll see how you do. Ready? 'A child watches too much television if he

1. can recognize an allusion to any commercial.
2. has seen more than one segment of *Masterpiece Theatre* [Here you insert the derisive comments of your choice on the order of "*Masterpiece Theatre,* the only decent show— remember the nights I've begged you to watch. Boy, if these people knew about the trash you kids. . . ."],
3. knows the brand name of any product [Here you hoot in contempt *ex tempore*],
4. ever asks with interest the time of day.' "

After you've tallied their scores, you launch into your sermon, giving special fervor to the peroration and the new rules of the house.

If you like television and your family carps about the lost hours of companionship and service, you can demonstrate your greater obligation with "An adult is culturally deprived if she/he does not know

1. that David Stewart has had amnesia on *As the World Turns,*

2. that Dan Rather has sixteen new ties (and   139
may also have had amnesia),

3. that Cal Worthington (who has not had
amnesia) presents for our viewing pleasure *Mrs.
Miniver, Waterloo Bridge, Camille, Casablanca,
Good Sam,* and hundreds of other classics we
can't claim to know unless we've seen them a
dozen times.

4. that all civilized people who have not had
amnesia can complete most of the lines in
M*A*S*H and can recite a full narrative of every
sports event ever televised."

As they say in government, the scenario is
wide open. A hearty eater can concoct a delicious
series of questions for "Are You Eating Enough
Rich Food?" Let the wastrel and the miser, the
fastidious and the slovenly, who are often
married to each other, come up with definitive
test after definitive test. Wanderers and stay-at-
homes, early risers and slug-a-beds (this pair
should read "hyperactive lunatics and God-fearing
defenders of all that is reasonable, honorable, and
good," but never mind), rowdies and dainties—all
of us can justify and condemn under the authority
of the test.

Dear Nanny

DEAR NANNY: I work hard and try to budget, but my wife is a grasshopper and I am an ant. Is there a service organization which could counsel us?

THRIFTY

DEAR THRIFTY: Immediately consult an entomologist at the nearest university. Your case should cause great excitement.

DEAR NANNY: My wife has decimated any respect I had for her by her sloppiness. Books, papers, and magazines are scattered on every surface in the house including kitchen counters. No amount of insisting and none of my dictums will make her pick up this clutter. I admit that I am conservative and that others may see her messiness as a charming bohemianism, but I cannot live much longer in this atmosphere.

HATES CLUTTER

DEAR HATES: Nanny too admits to being conservative, and she cannot hold with the newfangled sloppiness of strewing around "decimate" to mean "to destroy a large part of." As you should know by analogy to "decimal" if nothing else, "decimate" properly means "to take the tenth part of" or, more vividly, "to select by lot and punish with death every tenth man of; as to *decimate* a regiment for mutiny." Nanny respects a tidiness in forming plurals and cannot understand why people expect her to stumble over their clutter of "-ums" when she has insisted repeatedly that "-a" is usually correct. Nanny suggests that you refrain from littering the mails with "dictums."

DEAR NANNY: I am stunned. My husband of ten years has just told me that I am boring. We have a lovely house and two beautiful children, and I thought we were the perfect couple. How should I handle this situation?

STUNNED

DEAR STUNNED: Nanny cannot even fake an
interest in your problem.

DEAR NANNY: I left my wife when our daughter,
Louise, was an infant, and I have not seen them
since. Louise has written to ask me to give her
away at her wedding next month. I don't see
why I should have to go to the expense of
traveling across the country to attend the
wedding.

EX-FATHER

DEAR EX: If Louise is yours to give away, then
surely she is yours to sell. Brush up on
marketing techniques quickly, and make as much
money from the transaction as possible.

DEAR NANNY: I am horrified by the laziness of
people around me. They lie around like beached
whales watching television and accomplishing
nothing. We once were an industrious nation, but
now we don't use even one-tenth of. . . .

DEAR HORRIFIED: Stop right there. Nanny let
you get by with "beached whale," her candidate
for cliché of the decade, but she is not going to
subject herself to reading or hearing ever again
that we use only one-tenth of our brain. Nor will

144   Nanny allow anyone to refer to the percentage of an iceberg which is under or above water. She issues herewith a decree against any reference to elderly Eskimos abandoned on ice floes, the optimist who sees a glass half full, and a Chinese saying that if you save a man's life you become responsible for him.

DEAR NANNY: I am a ten-year-old girl interested in politics as a career. Would you list the names of all the female governors and senators from New Mexico?

LITTLE GIRL

DEAR LITTLE: No. Space does not permit.

DEAR NANNY: What is the criteria for a good marriage?

WANTS A WIFE

DEAR WANTS: A good marriage comes from knowing the difference between singular and plural. Being plural, "criteria" must have a plural verb. "These criteria are essential," but "This criterion is essential." Try other exercises: "These data are important," and "This datum is important"; "These media are driving people crazy," and "This medium is driving people

crazy"; "These strata of society are fortunate," 145
and "This stratum of society is fortunate." Nanny
doubts that any medium has equipped you with a
single criterion to find a datum on an unfortunate
or fortunate social stratum for lunch even at a
cafeterium.

DEAR NANNY: I can't get work and can't support
my children. Where can I go for help?

SINGLE MOTHER

DEAR SINGLE: The private sector will take care
of you. If you find its address, please let Nanny
know.

DEAR NANNY: I'm a good-looking, intelligent
man, but no one pays me the attention I
deserve. What's wrong?

DESERVES MORE

DEAR DESERVES: You are suffering from high
self-esteem.

DEAR NANNY: I'm smart, but I'm not getting
ahead in my line of work. Tell me, what counts—
what you know or who you know?

NO CONTACTS

Dear Nanny

DEAR NO: What counts with Nanny is knowing when to say "who" or "whom."

DEAR NANNY: Is it possible to get pregnant from swimming in a public pool?

WONDERING

DEAR WONDERING: Yes, indeedy. And from swallowing a watermelon seed and from using a pay telephone. Let Nanny know when you swell up. Nanny cares.

DEAR NANNY: A professional woman, I usually wear a string of pearls. Recently I acquired a necklace of emeralds set in gold. If I wore it, would it seem garish and undermine my image?

CORPORATE EXECUTIVE

DEAR CORPORATE: Stick with the pearls, dear. Send Nanny the emeralds, and she'll test them for a few months.

DEAR NANNY: I am a with-it guy, but my buddies and girls are uptight and repressed. I believe everyone should discuss their feelings the way I do, but they act strange when I tell about my

148   anger, frustration, jealousy, etc. How can I get
them to be honest with their emotions and let it
all hang out?

IN TOUCH

DEAR IN: Being singular, "everyone" requires a
singular pronoun. Your friends know that ideas
are inherently more interesting than feelings.
They doubtless care about the lively play of mind
and the exchange of observation, information, or
narrative. People have no compelling need to talk
about emotions: Affection, compassion,
enthusiasm, mirth, and generosity can be
enacted; anger, frustration, and jealousy can be
overcome. You are wrong to equate honesty with
self-indulgence. A recital of your feelings is less
gripping than an account of your hourly pulse
rate. Since you like to brood and seethe, for
heaven's sake spare everyone else. If the
converse of "uptight" is "downloose," then you
want to be especially careful *not* to "let it all hang
out." You are an embarrassment and a bore, but
Nanny will forgive if you'll promise to mend your
ways and mind your pronouns.

DEAR NANNY: I am interested in domestic
politics. How can I learn more about the way our
system works?

INTERESTED

DEAR INTERESTED: Try being poor.

Note: If you have a problem you want solved instantly, write NANNY. For a personal reply, enclose a stamped, self-addressed envelope and all your money.

Dressing for a Blessing

Not having attained the level of success that allows for leisure to study steps toward success, I rely upon trickle-down information. One friend recites the words of Dr. Joyce Brothers on getting whatever we want, and a slight acquaintance enjoins me to learn to win through intimidation. Because the last time I wanted to win anything was the day I missed "Dialing for Dollars" and as consolation ended up with a lifetime supply of Sta-Secures, winning as a way of life is as unthinkable as intimidation. On the bright side, *Machiavelli and Management* has a renaissance appeal, however perverse, and I adore the imperative to indolence behind *Think and Grow Rich.*

The latest rage to pass me by is a series of

152   instructions about dressing for success. At first I thought the message was to dress, simply to dress, a formula to avoid entering a meeting barefooted in a favorite venerable bathrobe as I have done. Instead, apparently the books tell exactly what to wear for power, for manipulation, for riches. Rather than spending the price of a new robe (and this one must look a fright by now) to buy them, I have conducted interviews of successful people.

1. Noted painter Foster McPherson readily boasts that he has sixty-one suits. No thrift store within driving range of his 1949 Ford pickup can stock an elaborate suit longer than a week. As impressive as the texture and cut of his coats are their linings, intense with the illusion of enamel work. With alarming realism, one lining portrays brook trout in eternally static strikes at lures, another scenes of bullfights, and another the flags of forty-eight states. On formal occasions McPherson wears in his lapel a wildflower or weed, but he scorns jewelry as "a pseudo-decorative obfuscation of linear purity."

Confident that a well-crafted suit makes its own
statement, he rejects the harsh geometric lines
of collar and tie, choosing the fluid arc of a T-
shirt. His tennis shoes announce the disparity
between form and function, and when very cold
weather calls for socks, their color and design
comment upon the cacophonous harmony
established by the oxymoronic equilibrium of his
ensemble, each part being a major voice rather
than a descant in the composition as gestalt.

2. Lotte Lester, author, speaker, and
supporter of causes, said, "I have my
Indian jewelry, and from there I wear
whatever is on top of the pile
on my closet floor." Urged to
discuss the selection of her
wardrobe, she replied,
"Heavens, I don't remember ever
buying clothes. It seems I've had
these always, but some may have
been gifts from family. To tell the
truth, if I thought I had a
wardrobe, I'd toss everything out
and make do with what I have on.
Real people don't have
wardrobes." At my admiration of
what appeared to be a Pop Art accessory to her
shawl, she disentangled a coathanger caught in

154   the fringes and wondered aloud how long it had been there. Asked about other favorite accessories, she remarked, "I have no idea what an accessory is, unless it's that old camel bladder I carry for a handbag."

3. Clarence Patterson, independent operator of a drilling supply and rig maintenance company, showed an immediate interest in clothes. "Hail, girl, I used to could wear what I had always wore—my boots and hat and Levis. But last year on a job up to Wink, Texas, bunch of ole boys beat me near to chicken-fried steak thankin I was some kind of northerner. You know, hon, them yankees eventual ruin everthang, and now they taken the clothes off our back. Sinct then I been pickin up these here tacky green outfits at Penny's or Monkey Ward's, don't matter which. Coleman feller give me this Caterpillar hat, plastic. Don't nobody but rattlers like shoes in the stead of boots. I look goofy all the time, but nobidy has mistook me for a yankee." I thought Mr. Patterson looked dashing

and said so. He reached in his truck and handed
me a Pearl beer from the cooler. "You caint beat
basic green and Pearls," he said.

4. Sandra Adams, economist and market
research analyst, designs and sews her own
clothes. "Oil cloth, everything is made from oil
cloth. I don't trust people who wear beige linen.
It shows they don't spill food or have pets or
write with ink. They don't live." Adams this day
presented an arresting sight in a school-bus
yellow A-frame dress. "Don't be
afraid to stand out. Be timid, and
you'll be overlooked. This fabric
lasts forever, and I just hose
it down at night. Oil cloth."
Catching my surreptitious
glance at her feet, she said,
"Durability! These shoes I've
had fifteen years and will have
for fifteen more. Every year I
put on new soles. You don't
know what they're made of,
do you?" I knew, but managed
to look quizzical. "An old tire
costs $1.50 and keeps me in
soles for ten years." "And your purse?" I
hazarded. "Aha, that's one secret I won't

156   divulge." It looked like an armadillo shell wrapped
       in baling wire. "Remember my rules: easy
       cleaning, durability, and nothing timid. The only
       women who spend money on clothes are working
       for minimum wage."

Get a Tuffet

More strident and confident in righteousness than the Moral Majority are those who proclaim the new morality of physical fitness. Boasting as they adjust their Ace bandages, they proselytize by scolding and prophesying doom to the lethargic. Their livid depictions of the torments awaiting those of us whose minds wander momentarily from rigorous heart-lung maintenance or arterial clarity make the hell of Jonathan Edwards seem like a multi-starred Michelin hotel.

Not yet a member of this majority of physical rectitude, neither am I of the minority who take pride in indolence. I confess that by nature, experience, and habit I know that lolling and dawdling bring greater pleasure than huffing and splinting and spraining, and empirical evidence shows that a hammock is safer than a playing field. Certainly nothing we have to stand up to do is worth doing. I have Biblical sanction too: "For bodily exercise profiteth little" (1 Timothy 4:8).

Still, I probably would be an enthusiastic, possibly great, athlete were it not for the pedagogy of physical activity. Any course of instruction I have undertaken to enrich blood circulation or improve muscle tone has turned humiliating and offensive because of the arrogance of instructors. Their favorite teaching tools are mocking, maligning, cursing, and threatening.

My first tennis lesson deflected hopes of a life of vigorous and elegant exercise when the despot-teacher, in a manic and cruel charade of my strokes, broke my new racquet while shouting to the class that I looked like a poster child for the Flailing Elbow Foundation. The next tennis coach made me gather balls for six weeks while he practiced his game and admonished me to watch his form and despair that I could ever aspire to perfection. The last wore five happy-face buttons and tried to berate me into accepting Scientology before we could move on to tennis.

The tyranny of instructors is matched only by the docility of their students. If the teacher says,

"Get a tuffet and sit on it," every pupil scavenges
to find one for a perch. Anyone involved in
nonphysical education knows another form of
student-teacher exchange. At every state
university professors are cooing a variation of
this paradigm: "Robert, I noticed quite by chance
that in your paper you say, 'I have did,' 'them
what has went,' and 'more worriersomer than all
of we.' These are charming regionalisms, and you
don't want to lose your individual voice, but when
you argue before the Supreme Court or accept
your Pulitzer Prize you will want to have a choice
among ways of speaking. All we want to do is
increase your options." Robert protests and
swears to have his lawyer sue for abuse. At the
same time, the physical pedants receive adulation
from those they call dummies, dingbats, idiots,
scum.

Heaven and earth (and I should couple hell)
know that I am not a difficult student. Dutifully I
buy all suggested equipment, I arrive fresh-faced
and eager, and I pay attention. Mockery and
calumny I can take, being used to it from my
friends and family, but the academicians of the
physical are genuinely committed to despising the
beginner and the inquiring mind. After two windy,
cold days of having a ski instructor point a pole at
me in disgust and scream to the entire Rocky
Mountain region, "Look at Mary Beth! Just do

the opposite of everything she does," I asked for an explanation of "unweighting," a miracle we had been ordered to perform. Physics I didn't require, nor did I want an exact definition, but looking down the mountain I did have gravity on my mind and bottom and needed either elementary advice or metaphysics. The instructor raged, "unweighting is unweighting, and if you don't like it you know what you can do with it." I didn't know at all what to do with it, so I murmured "tautology" and unweighted down the slope and out of the class, bruising fifty-two parts of my body along the way.

Yoga seemed a relaxing, noncompetitive exercise that incorporated body, mind, and spirit, so I enrolled in a class and attended with my mat, ludicrous costume, and holistic willingness to learn. I endured several weeks of ridicule: "Mary Bell, can't you keep up with everyone else and loop those toes around those ears? Everyone hates a nonelastic body and a person who won't even try to keep up." Hardly the meditative haven of serenity I had envisioned, this class aimed to grate, demoralize, and destroy. Having already broken a tooth clenching my jaws through command after command to "lay down," I ended my career as Lotus Blossom by obeying when the commandant screamed, "Lay prone." I did, and she shrieked, "Mary Lou, I said to lay prone." "I am," I said, skirting the verb. "Lay prone like everyone else!" "*I* am prone. Everyone else is supine," I said, proud of my assertion. As I recall, the yoga-master and the whole class, believing that "supine" describes the baser actions of creatures in an off-limits section of a zoo, turned on me. Maybe a Protestant shouldn't toy with the mysteries of the Orient.

Recently I ran into my boss, the president of the University of New Mexico. I asked, "How was your trip to China, Bud?" (I call him Bud.) "Well, Mary Jane," he said, "the most interesting information I picked up about higher education there is that the faculty all do calisthenics together at sunrise." Since he's jovial, I said, "If this is your way of handing out pink slips, I accept mine." He chuckled, I think, and said, "All right, Mary Ann, I'll remember that."

As I wait for him to remember and release me to toil in the fields, my arteries are clogging, my vital signs are working on being less vital, and I'm enjoying the freedom from despotism promised us by our founding mothers and fathers. Until the reform of pedagogy in physical fitness, we can lie supine, ignore our elbows, and keep our eyes on a book instead of the ball.

The New Yellow Peril

Many people who give their newspapers cursory reading may have overlooked the small headline: "Soviets Breeding Canaries That Can Sing Bass."

On the surface the information suggests that the Soviet Union has leapt decades ahead of us culturally. I once heard a recording of American canaries singing, appropriately, "Listen to the Mockingbird." Though earnest, their rendition was pained and tweeted, lacking the full-throated resonance one expects of the Soviet chorus. The American choir had one point in its favor: the birds sounded as if they were free, not caged but standing in little rows, straining on tiptoe to follow their conductor, a cardinal maybe. But the group included only sopranos, and not a

164   coloratura in the bunch. Musicologists tell me
that after this effort the United States abandoned
artistic progress with canaries, probably because
of Senator Proxmire.

We must look behind the broad aesthetic
implications to the subtler scientific ones. The
Soviets are not simply training voices, nor are
they injecting individual canaries full to the gills (I
took biology a long time ago) with testosterone
to lower the voice. They are *breeding* canaries to
vocal ranges. They are producing whole
generations of basses. This process is more
complex than mixing primary colors. What
results, for example, when a bass mates with an
alto is surely not a nestful of tenor eggs.
Something lurks here that should alert our
genetic engineers.

So the USSR is flying ahead both culturally and
scientifically. That's what they want us to think.
But think again. Art and science are merely
blinds to their true endeavor. Think harder.
Review your nightmares. Consider what might
finally unsettle your mind forever. For the sake
of the entire Free World, here is the news
account:

MOSCOW (AP) Ornithologists in the Soviet
Ukraine have bred canaries able to sing bass for a
canary singing group whose repertoire includes

Beethoven's "Moonlight Sonata" and Russian folk
songs, the newspaper Moscow News reported.

The paper said the canaries, trained by former
stagehand Fedor Fomenko, already include sopranos,
tenors, and other vocal ranges.

My friend the actress who is uninformed about
current events loftily dismisses the whole matter
with "What can a stagehand know of breeding?"
But take note, America. This development is a
MILITARY move, part of the Soviet global
strategy, as serious as germ warfare.

Whole communities could be changed, not that

166   you'd notice in some, to hell-pits of appalling horror with crazed citizens running through the streets, all commerce halted, armies immobilized. Those patriots who own guns would point them toward themselves. We may see our nation undone by troops of canaries, plumed Chaliapins, marching through our arteries to the hearts of our great cities, from sea to shining sea, from the mountains to the prairie. Some of us will break under the "Moonlight Sonata," others from weeks of Russian folk songs. Cats, our natural defense, will cower before a basso profundo every time.

The State Department and the Pentagon, sensitive nowadays to any Slavic sneeze, should have caught this warning. They must immediately devise a retaliatory system whereby at the first sight of an alien wing we pipe into every apartment and dacha in the Soviet Union the squeals of our game-show contestants.

Twenty-Three Pomeranians

Last winter as I was completing an elaborate paint-by-number landscape, there came a sudden image of a friend I had not seen in many years. Although others occasionally told me of his travels and his life in a distant city, we had not corresponded. At that moment I saw him vividly, several years older than when we had last met, tanned, with an unfamiliar but not unattractive scar beside his left eye. He was dressed conservatively for him, in fawn corduroy, and, while keeping his intense gaze and alertness, he showed a new compassion. I felt as if he were standing before me, and the sensation remained for ten minutes.

The clarity of the vision caused me to clean

168 my brush, and wanting to shake the apparition, I
drove to a park in an out-of-the-way section of
town. I had never been to this park, but I felt
guided to it by a strange force. An old Spanish
woman was selling flowers that do not bloom in
winter—narcissus, violets, and daffodils.
Bordering the lawn, oleanders and lilacs were in
full flower. A young couple danced to exotic
music, as another played Parcheesi. Twenty-
three Pomeranians ran free with no apparent
owner. Dachshunds were everywhere, digging
and snuffling. Like the flowers, none of the dogs
was in season.

Because of the chilly though sunny day I was
bundled up, but soon I removed my parka,
sweaters, cap, and mittens and sat comfortably in
my yellow pinafore with the eyelet flounce. In
that spot I was certain I would see no one I
knew.

To my surprise, directly toward me walked a
woman who five years before had retired from
the reference department at the library. She
didn't recognize me and passed by. Her pinafore
was exactly like mine, but lime green, a
Butterick pattern!

Night fell quickly. I returned home and filled in
the seventy-sixes on my painting and made a
waffle. The very next month I heard indirectly

that the friend in my vision had undergone surgery for heel spurs!

Surely truth is stranger than non-truth, and we understand only dimly the wondrous phenomena of the mind.

Perchance to Think of Something Else

Dozing off can be one of life's simplest
pleasures. In a lecture hall or warm theater sleep
often comes irresistibly, but at bedtime the brain
can be overactive and recalcitrant and downright
ornery.

Seeking sleep at bedtime carries its rituals,
chiefly a litany of worries. Mine begin humbly
with chores undone, the reluctance of heaven to
guarantee the health, happiness, and immortality
of family, friends, and pets, and then they spread
to world hunger, mutability, inhumanity,
possibilities of planetary devastation, human
suffering past, present, and future. After some
hours I go directly to immediate concerns: The
bone necklace from Peru given to me by a
cherished friend in the Peace Corps must be

172   somewhere, but I've looked in every cranny over
the years. My left stereo (now mono) speaker
still won't work after I paid more than its value in
dollars and certainly in humiliation taking it to the
shop and admitting that my dog, Bubba Anaya,
had eaten its large round section. "HO HO HO
HO," the repairman shouted to the store at large
before he announced just what I had hoped to
circumlocute: "Her DOG ate her WOOFER! Her
canary will eat the tweeter. HO HO HO."
Continuing my counterproductive prelude to
sleep, I plot a return to the repair shop. In this
version I am authoritative and announce in the
way of business and dissatisfaction that the
speaker doesn't speak. Someone (probably the
loud man, Gary) calls out, "She's back. Here's
the lady whose dog ate her woofer." For relief I
return to fretting about the future of our planet

and the greed and ignorance of the
administration. As dawn does her rosy-fingered
act, I sink back to worries about chores undone,
the lack of a guarantee for the health and
happiness of family, friends, and pets, and begin
to recycle.

174   In an aberrant moment of clarity, I realized
that in Albuquerque, New Mexico, in the middle
of the night I couldn't solve world hunger, locate
a necklace, repair Bubba's speaker, safeguard my
family, or right the wrongs of any government. In
early adulthood I learned that personal financial
woes are not soporific, but only now can I
prohibit a host of topics for bedtime and
recommend instead special fabricated worries.
Aiming to avoid a dark night of the soul or even a
gloaming of the soul and realizing that thoughts
need work in order to wind down and let dreams
take over, we merely supplant one set of cares
with another.

Forbid yourself to think of money, nations,
anyone twenty-one or younger, anyone twenty-
one or older, the past, present, or future,
chores, repairs, your funeral, your adolescence,
the condition of your health, car, roof, heating,
electrical, or plumbing systems, others' lack of
health, car, roof, heating, electrical, or plumbing
systems, or reasons you have to apologize or
feel remiss. "Ought," "should," "must," and
"thank-you notes" do not belong in slumber's
lexicon. Comparing yourself with another has the
effect of caffeine, and the slightest thought of
Mother Teresa works like amphetamines.
Never plan an exercise program, resolve to

change bad habits, or wonder how you have ever slept with your arm and shoulder as unwieldy as tree trunks and the clock more percussive than a parade in River City.

When fabricating safe topics, avoid those involving knowledge or memory. A sure way to greet the milkman is to try to remember a melody, title, or name. I might as well sit up, turn on the lights, and remove my eyelids as review what I know about Jutland or the way clams breed or petty details of the Boer War (such as who fought whom where and why) or the identity of Procris. My nighttime excursions into science begin with curious confidence, lead to research through the entire Golden Book series, and end in plans to go back to school. "What's that law called, the one about a submerged object which displaces water equal to, equal to something? It's somebody's name. Water equal to what? weight, bulk, exchange in pounds sterling?"

Slumber-effective worries tested by my renowned laboratory allow the mind temperate activity but do not invite real thought, emotions, or memory. Safe ones for beginners include:

1. What if the sky were green and the grass cerise?

2. In what ways would the world be different without glass or mirrors?

3. What is the best scent on earth? Is wisteria superior to cloves? Be careful not to link any scent with a setting, person, or event.

4. What single food are you gladdest to have? Usually I drift off while orange juice and home-grown tomatoes fight it out, but, since nobody is monitoring, you can without remorse give the battle over to radish tops and Elmer's glue.

5. If you could go anywhere in the world for three months, but to one place only, where would you go? Do not include memories, people, ambition, disappointed hopes. Always keep your inner eye on the object.

6. Assume that either Bach or Shakespeare had never been born. You decide which one. This topic is on the intermediate level because danger lies in constructing variants. If you posit that Shakespeare was too down in the dumps to write *Hamlet* or that Bach was too busy to set down the *Mass* or that either was too lazy to do much of anything, then soon you'll be applying matters to yourself. You're better off letting one of them be unconceived or born female.

Born female! Somewhere in this house I know I have two old sleeping pills. Maybe they lose their potency after several years. I wonder who coined the term "shelf-life," and tomorrow I'll check the etymology of "shelf," but then I never do anything I ought to do, and I don't have time to do what I want, and the whole mess is a problem of my own making, and what kind of dope-head would remember two sleeping pills stashed away years ago? If I took one, then I'd probably move on to harder stuff and do even less for the health and happiness of family, friends, the world. Foolish stuff, thinking I could find a pill when I can't imagine where to look for the necklace from Peru. Sunrise already? Aurora herself. And what are the other names for dawn? I ought to know.

Thank You for Your Letter

The latest demographic indicators and weather
reports alert us to a migration to the Southwest.
Most of us who have been here over twenty
minutes are ready to slam the doors of entry.

As a pioneer mother, I am taking action. At
night I sneak into the offices of the Chamber of
Commerce and answer letters. Here are the
ones I mailed this morning.

1.

Thank you for your interest in living amid the
three cultures of New Mexico. You will be happy
to know that you can explore freely the
ceremonies of all three: Presbyterian, Methodist,
and Episcopal. Despite their denominational
disparities, they display a homogeneity unknown

180   in any other part of the nation. In our fair state
we proudly look alike, we watch the same
television shows, we eat the same foods, and,
most important, we think alike.

Your question about native Americans made us
do some surveying, and we found that all of us
are native Americans except for a few Slavic
people who keep to themselves and some Texans
who make trouble for everyone else.

2.

Thank you for your letter inquiring about
recreational activities in this area. You and your
family will find it an invigorating environment with
its whist tournaments, meetings of the Louisa
May Alcott Guild, and numerous early music
ensembles, all of which will welcome you. Our
Chamber files contain scanty materials about
camping, since the parks around the state have
recently been paved, to the regret of no one.

Frankly, people here don't often venture
outside, and those who do are clothed like
beekeepers because of the constant high winds
and dust storms and because New Mexico
proudly boasts attaining third place, behind
Australia and New Zealand, in the incidence of
skin cancer. The Chamber staff found under
"hiking" only one item: A philately society some
years ago organized a parade in celebration of a

new issue on Arbor Day or some such, resulting
in several fatalities and bad will all around.

Don't let any of this information deter you
from making the move. You and your family, if
heavily insured, can enjoy driving our
sophisticated freeways and viewing our urban and
industrial growth.

3.

Received this day your letter inquiring about
real estate values. I have good news for you. If
you are willing to curtail the wasteful and
ostentatious caricature of a life-style you
describe, you can settle in one of our finest
tarpaper residences for a nominal amount, say
$800,000 for 600 of the most commodious square
feet east of Kingman, not counting the exclusive
private facility (24 square feet) out back.

Your question about utilities is a puzzler, but I
figure about three dollars a month for kerosene
or coal oil if you stay up late. If you don't bring
your own wood to burn for heat, you'll be up a
creek, if there were one, since somebody
chopped down the last tree in the state about
twenty years ago.

Act soon, since competition for housing is stiff.
Our local realtor is wintering in Fargo, but when
she returns I'll ask her to write you.

4.

You have certainly chosen the right place to live! Your fears will melt away in our tranquil village.

Though I do not leave home without armor and weapons, inside the compound I feel perfectly secure. In fact, my only complaint is that since we equipped our living unit with world-premier lights, attack dogs, and an arsenal, my household goods need repair. No longer can we count on replacing the stereo and television sets every few weeks, so the wear is showing.

My children play freely in our many parks without my having to worry. I believe only two or three have disappeared recently—well, maybe four, counting the 15-year-old, but you never know what kind of mischief they're up to at that age.

In answer to your question about schools, all I can tell you is that every teacher I know looks haggard and spent. The men who work the concession stands surrounding the schoolyards are cheerful and polite during their daily grind of dealing dope to children too young to make change.

We look forward to welcoming you to the serenity of the high desert. You ask for advice, but not much is needed. Just remember: After

you shoot an intruder, pull the body inside your
house.

5.

What a pleasure to welcome to New Mexico "a
woman of fashion, a dealer of finer cosmetics,
and a model," as you describe yourself! You will
enjoy the energetic commerce here, although you
may want to change the wares you peddle.
Because of our humidity, which usually hovers
around three (it did shoot up to fourteen on
November 16, 1924), nearly everyone here just
greases up with lard, but the opulent and self-
conscious reportedly go for specialty items such
as Crisco and ChapStick. You will be pleased to
know that the climate etches lines of character,
experience, and suffering that even our youngest
women wear with pride.

A recent editorial in our local newspaper
pertains to your other professions: "We expect
our ladyfolk to work the fields and stock right
along with the menfolk, and if she don't she's run
out on a rail straight back to where she come
from."

When you arrive, please let us know, since we
can assist you in hastening your order for
evening wear from Red Wing and Wrangler. As a
favor woman-to-woman, would you please bring

me a bar of Lifebuoy soap? I've been using Lava
or Boraxo for so long I've forgotten what luxury
is like.

6.

Please excuse the delay in answering your
letter. All our staff have been laid up for a month
because somehow the pollen finds its way
through the blowing snow and sleet. But soon
spring will come, bringing the delicate blossoms
of ragweed and goldenrod and other fresh signs
of rebirth which hearten everyone who is not
struck down by Elm Fever. Then we'll enjoy the
pleasures of 112 degrees for several months.

You should come here right away to escape
that bad weather up there. Your wife will feel
better immediately since this area can give her
the best treatment; 80 percent of our physicians
are allergists, and they make life possible for
most of us.

We'll be especially glad to have you working in
construction. The only house started here last
year never got past the framing stage because no
one was fool enough to work on it, and we'd like
to see it finished.

7.

The Chamber of Commerce and the whole
community look forward to the arrival of such an

enterprising and creative talent as you, Johnny
Flash. We are seeking someone with your
experience in the entertainment world.

Your letter arrived at the very moment we had
news of exactly the opportunity you need, and
we expect you to prosper as we benefit. For a
tad more than you say you are willing to invest
you can purchase K-DED, our around-the-clock
obituary station!

You will have hardly any competition, and with
a little promotional work you can have a hefty
percentage of all crystal sets in range tuned to
K-DED.

Call our office immediately, and you can pick
up this station for a song, or dirge, as it were.
When you call, ask for me, since K-DED belongs
to the estate of my late great-aunt's cousin, and I
am the executrix. FCC rulings, of course, do not
apply to New Mexico, so we are free to
negotiate. I will ask nothing beyond the sale price
than a third of the gross and full editorial control.

8.

Today with much merriment we read your
letter scrawled in pencil on what appears to be a
page torn from a Big Chief tablet and signed
"Girlene and Buck." We at the Chamber have not
witnessed such gaucherie since at the White
House the Queen of England was made to

186 endure a rendition of "Muskrat Love."

To be candid, Mr. and Mrs. Buck, we cannot imagine that you would find Albuquerque to your taste or you to ours. We spend our time with our furriers, accountants, or jewelers, and the only employment opportunities here are for investors, candy stripers, or docents.

You inquire about school lunches. We can only assume that they consist of what any civilized person has at noon—a good Pouilly-Fuissé and Brie with fruit.

9.

Sure appreciate your letter telling about your life in a high-rise apartment building and how you want to move here even if you know about us only through book reading. We're mighty proud you and your large family are coming here, and I'm glad you don't have the usual finicky questions about housing, jobs, taxes, climate (which we fib about to the Weather Bureau), and schools.

Yessir, you have picked the right place "to maintain your urban life in a pleasant climate and to enjoy a lively cosmopolitan center," as you say. You'll find the busy life at the post office or the grocery during the summer, when the snow isn't so high, or down at the feed store—man down there has a parrot can talk. And for

cosmopolitan, we had a feller and the wife in
from San Antone last month and some folks out
of Bakersfield a year ago, real interesting talkers
except the San Antone woman done away with
the county treasury box.

We got a lot to brag about that your books
don't tell. By proclamation of the governor and
unanimal consent of what legislators was present
on hand to cast votes, the State Insect is the
scorpion or vinegarroon, the State Bird the
vulture, the State Snake the desert rattler (and
you got to watch them critters, come right into a
eighteenth-floor condominial), the State Spider
the brown recluse (snuggled into the collars of
your shirts and in pajamas straight from the
wash), and, so proudly we hail, the State Disease
is the plague, two varieties. The State Motto is
"Stranger, Do Not Enter Through These
Portals." Welcome to the Land of Enchantment!

The End